Zbigniew Drozdowicz

Standards of Philosophical Rationality

Development in Humanities

edited by

Zbigniew Drozdowicz
(General Editor)

and Sławomir Sztajer

Volume 1

LIT

Zbigniew Drozdowicz

Standards
of Philosophical Rationality

Traditions and Modern Times

LIT

NARODOWY PROGRAM
ROZWOJU HUMANISTYKI

The present thesis has been financed as a part of a programme of the Ministry of Science and Higher Education, which is called: the National Programme for the Development of Humanities (NPRH)

Typesetting by Michał Staniszewski

This book is printed on acid-free paper.

Bibliographic information published by the Deutsche Nationalbibliothek
The Deutsche Nationalbibliothek lists this publication in the Deutsche Nationalbibliografie; detailed bibliographic data are available in the Internet at http://dnb.d-nb.de.

ISBN 978-3-643-90388-4

A catalogue record for this book is available from the British Library

©LIT VERLAG GmbH & Co. KG Wien, Zweigniederlassung Zürich 2013
Klosbachstr. 107
CH-8032 Zürich
Tel. +41 (0) 44-251 75 05
Fax +41 (0) 44-251 75 06
E-Mail: zuerich@lit-verlag.ch
http://www.lit-verlag.ch

LIT VERLAG Dr. W. Hopf
Berlin 2013
Fresnostr. 2
D-48159 Münster
Tel. +49 (0) 2 51-62 03 20
Fax +49 (0) 2 51-23 19 72
E-Mail: lit@lit-verlag.de
http://www.lit-verlag.de

Distribution:
In Germany: LIT Verlag Fresnostr. 2, D-48159 Münster
Tel. +49 (0) 2 51-620 32 22, Fax +49 (0) 2 51-922 60 99, E-mail: vertrieb@lit-verlag.de

In Austria: Medienlogistik Pichler-ÖBZ, e-mail: mlo@medien-logistik.at
In Switzerland: B + M Buch- und Medienvertrieb, e-mail: order@buch-medien.ch
In the UK: Global Book Marketing, e-mail: mo@centralbooks.com
In North America: International Specialized Book Services, e-mail: orders@isbs.com
e-books are available at www.litwebshop.de

Contents

Author's note

Attempts at indicating philosophical standards (models) of rationality are connected with a philosophy that would aspire to be more than simply wisdom arising from current human needs and responding to those needs – for does someone living only in the present moment and caring only to satisfy his immediate needs deserve to be called a true philosopher? Philosophy has not yet focused on this rhetorical question, but rather searched for standards that would indicate the path to philosophical rationality for anyone who is willing and able to evaluate and appreciate them. The problem lies not only within the variety of opinions about this path amongst philosophers, but it is also in the fact that this object of philosophical desire, the goal of the journey along the path, has presented itself differently, or at least was differently named and described by them. Obviously, these differences did not always entail the impossibility of reaching such an agreement that would have an effect on the indication of certain constant elements of rationality, or at least ones about which we could credibly say that they are repeated with a regularity within the different standards of rationality, which allows them to be considered as the *rules* without which none of the standards of rationality occurring in philosophy could do without.

One such common element of the standards of rationality proposed in the past was the concept of *rule* itself. Like many other fundamental philosophical concepts, it derives from Greek (*ἀρχή*). Many Greek philosophers used it, and an attempt at defining it was made by Aristotle in his *Prior and Posterior Analytics*. Already within the opening lines of this work he mentioned the following: the rule of demonstrative (deductive) reasoning, the rule of non-contradiction and the rule of syllogism.[1] Later in the work, Aristotle follows with: the rule of definition, the rule of proof, the rule of conversion, the rule of reduction,

---

[1] "A syllogism is discourse in which, certain things being stated, something other than what is stated follows of necessity from their being so." Cf. Aristotle, *Works*, Oxford 1956, p. 81.

the rule of contradiction etc. Also, he provides a definition of his concept of rules ("I call rules, in each case, those statements which cannot be proved") and lists different kinds of rules, including the distinction of *the prior rules*.[2]

Undoubtedly, Aristotle within this work is a master of logical order, including passing from the general to the particular, and from the particular to the general. Let us quote the final paragraph of this work here, as it contains a synthesis of Aristotelian thinking on *rules*. Here he says that: "no other kind of thought except intuition is more accurate than scientific knowledge, whereas primary premisses are more knowable than demonstrations, and all scientific knowledge is discursive. From these considerations it follows that there will be no scientific knowledge of the primary premisses, and since except intuition nothing can be truer than scientific knowledge, it will be intuition that apprehends the primary premisses – a result which also follows from the fact that demonstration cannot be the origination source of demonstration, nor, consequently, scientific knowledge of scientific knowledge. If, therefore, it is the only other kind of true thinking except scientific knowing, intuition will be the origination source of scientific knowledge. And the originative source of science grasps the original basic premiss, while science as a whole is similarly related as originative source to the whole body of fact."[3] Although not everything in this opinion is completely lucid, it is clear that according to this philosopher intellectual intuition is *the mother of rules*. At a later time this conviction was shared by some philosophers, but questioned by others.

In the past, another common element of different standards of rationality was the concept of *reason*. This concept coming from the Latin *ratio* was not only to be a complement for the Greek concept of *rule* (in a particular case its equivalent), but also its extension – meaning both *reason* as well as *mind, account, reference, relation, manner, state* etc. To this differentiation, another one was added, i.e., one distinguishing *reason* into *satisfactory* and *sufficient, determining* and *justifying, ordering* and *explaining* etc.[4] The great rationalists of modern and most recent times such as Descartes, Kant, Hegel, Poincaré and Popper were capable of adding *reason* to this list, which did not fit within the standards of the rationality of their predecessors and so they founded new standards. Apart from all this, it means that there is a need to take a closer look at what they

---

[2] "Of the basic truths used in the demonstrative sciences some are peculiar to each science, and some are common, but common only in the sense of analogous, being of use only in so far as they fall within the genus constituting the province of the science in question." Ibidem, p. 241.

[3] Ibidem, p. 325.

[4] Cf. B. Paź, *Naczelna zasada racjonalizmu. Od Kartezjusza do wczesnego Kanta*, Cracow 2007, p. 37 ff.

adopted and proposed, since only on this basis can one venture to answer the question of what the specificity of philosophical rationality and the changes occurring within it have consisted of – both then and now. Certainly, the depiction of rationality outlined in this dissertation does not render all its shades and hues, and it does not even show the whole palette of those which appear in the views of the philosophers discussed here. It does not render and cannot render them in all their complexity since the greatness of philosophers and philosophy consists in that not everything can be fully encompassed by the intellect and imagination of only one man.

Chapter I

Ancient traditions

1. Socrates

Certainly, ancient philosophy neither begins nor ends with Socrates (469-399 BCE). This philosopher, however, is in many ways considered to be a monumental figure, since he was the heir to that philosophical wisdom which had appeared in Greek philosophy before him; also, he had a fundamental influence on the philosophical thinking which came after him – even though he wrote nothing, and everything we know about him and his philosophy comes from so-called "second-hand" sources. It should be made clear that these relations differ substantially from each other, yet, obviously, some pieces of information in them are consistent. These, however, concern his philosophy to a lesser extent, but rather are more informative about his life. Therefore, we know when and where he lived – Diogenes Laertius in his *Lives and Opinions of Eminent Philosophers* states that Socrates was born and spent most of his life in Athens.[1] We also know how he lived – the same author wrote that he lived modestly, but was also "a contented and venerable man" who "prided himself upon the simplicity of his life; and never exacted any pay from his pupils" for his teachings, which he gave to all who wanted to listen to him, and these were few (there were more of those who criticized him and even mocked him). We also know how he died and what the circumstances of his death were. We know these things because they were presented by one of his closest and most eminent friends, Plato (c. 428-347 BCE), in his *Apology of*

---

[1] "[He was] a pupil of Anaxagoras, as some people say," and "after the condemnation of Anaxagoras, he became a disciple of Archelaus, the natural philosopher." Cf. Diogenes Laertius, *Lives and Opinions of Eminent Philosophers*, London 1895, p. 64 ff.

Socrates.[2] From Plato's report it follows that Socrates gave his life for truth, or more precisely, for his courage in asking questions and seeking answers, as well as encouraging others to follow the same path.

These and other circumstances of his life contributed to the creation of a legend, which in philosophy recorded the image of a man and philosopher whose life wisdom (rationality) rose above the wisdom of his contemporaries, and that of many generations that followed him. This combination of wisdom with practical life is one of the most important components of the Socratic standard of rationality. Of course, it was not only Socrates' contribution. In fact, the same standard appears in different pre-Socratic schools, including the one in which he studied, that is, the Sophist school. Let us recall, then, that Sophists gave the concept of *sophoi* (wisdom, rationality) its personalistic, relativistic, individualistic, common sense and practical character.[3] Assessing their contribution to philosophy, Giovanni Reale writes that "All the Sophists aroused and variously analyzed moral problems and problems structurally connected with morality, but *they did not achieve, on the thematic level, the principle from which all could be derived.* [...] None of the Sophists has expressly stated, that is, thematically, what man is and consequently none of the Sophists was able to see consciously that the various doctrines that they professed united in a determined conception of man."[4] Generally, none of them expressed it because they believed that not even the greatest sage was able to express it, and that true wisdom (rationality) consists in not speaking that which cannot be said wisely (reasonably). This also is a part of Socratic rationality.

More information about Socrates can be deduced from what was provided by Diogenes Laertius in his *Lives and Opinions of Eminent Philosophers*. Among other things, he says there that the famous philosopher "was a man able to look down upon any who mocked him," and even endured with patience and forbearance acts of aggression from those whom his lifestyle drove to real fury ("he was treated with great violence and beaten, and pulled about").[5] One

---

[2] In the light of this report, Socrates was accused (by a man named Melitus) of "[acting] wickedly, and [being] criminally curious in searching into things under the earth, and in the heavens, and in making the worse appear the better cause, and in teaching these same things to others." Cf. Plato, *The Apology of Socrates*, in: *Plato's Apology, Crito and Phaedo*, Philadelphia 1897, p. 16 ff.

[3] "Previously, *sophia* meant those abilities which were connected with practical application, but also required significant wisdom; therefore, true wisdom is ultimately ability, and true ability is knowing how to bring to the open true quality, and efficiency is the measure of ability and wisdom as knowledge. [...] Wise is he who succeeds in everything." R. Elberfeld, *Was ist Philosophie? Programmatische Texte von Platon bis Derrida*, Stuttgart 2006, p. 19 ff.

[4] G. Reale, *A History of Ancient Philosophy. I: From the Origins to Socrates*, Albany 1987, p. 189.

[5] However, he held his contemporary Sophists (such as Prodicus of Ceos) in disregard. This was due to, among other things, the transformation of sophism into eristic, the art of

can surmise that this rage, ridicule and contempt on the part of his opponents was regarded by him as a manifestation of a lack of rationality on their part, or – what was just the same – a sign of being guided not by reason but by emotions. But, among other things, he tried to convince those who wanted to listen to him "that to begin well was not a trifling thing, but yet not far from a trifling thing; and that he knew nothing, except the fact of his ignorance. Another saying of his was that those who bought things out of season, at an extravagant price, expected never to live till the proper season for them. Once, when he was asked what was the virtue of a young man, he said, 'To avoid excess in everything.'" This moderation in all things is also a kind of hallmark of Socratic rationalism.

From the perspective of those who would like to find answers to questions about human existence, this is, of course, no great wisdom. However, it reflects the capacity of a person with a great life experience, and who can deduce from it a lesson for himself and for others, and is convinced that with every next step in his life, he will be even wiser (more rational). In this sense Socrates is a Sophist, i.e. someone who has gained wisdom and is willing to share and capable of sharing it with others. At least such is his image outlined by Plato.[6] Of course, Plato was neither the first nor the last to idealize his master and teacher. In this particular case of idealization, Socrates appears to be a sophisticated intellectual, as he is presented by another sophisticated intellectual, in the person of Plato. Yet this Socrates puts more emphasis on the intellect than on common sense, and he gets rid of those Sophistic doubts that made Sophists tend to ask questions and put question marks, rather than to adopt such solutions from which various kinds of essences of things would emerge.

In modern times such an idealized image of Socrates was presented by the author of *Lectures on the History of Philosophy* and master of the art of dialectical thinking, and – as some historians of philosophy claimed – the last great rationalist in philosophy, G. W. F. Hegel (1770-1831).[7] It is worth taking a slightly closer look at this idealization, as it pointed to an opposition fundamental to any rationalization, that is, the opposition between the rationality of negation and the rationality of affirmation. They form a pair which is sometimes mutually exclusive and sometimes complementary. However, most often they create a pair, which is complementary through their exclusion and

---

providing false claims with a semblance of truth. This is also mentioned by Diogenes Laertius in his work. Cf. Diogenes Laertius, *Lives and Opinions...*, op. cit., p. 64 ff.

[6] Giovanni Reale writes that Plato's "Socrates is a moral hero, he is a secular saint, strong, temperate, wise, just, the most authentic educator of men, the only true statesman that Athens has ever possessed;" he also adds that "Plato places in Socrates's mouth almost all of his own doctrines..." G. Reale, *A History of Ancient Philosophy. I: From the Origins...*, op. cit., p. 195.

[7] Cf. H. Schnädelbach, *Próba rehabilitacji animal rationale*, Warsaw 2001, p. 37 ff.

in each case remains in close relation with one another. According to Hegel, this already appears in the sentences of the so-called Seven Sages [Seven Wise Men of Greece] such as, e.g., Bias of Priene (b. ca. 570 BCE), author of the saying "Speak of the Gods as they are" (rationality of affirmation), and think of their existence as you want (rationality of negation), or Cleobulus (b. ca 600 BCE), who was said to have offered the following advice: "not to chastise a servant while elated with drink" (rationality of affirmation), "for so doing one will appear to be drunk one's self" (rationality of affirmation and rationality of negation at the same time). An even more complex structure is a seemingly simple saying of Socrates: "I know that I know nothing." It is difficult to indicate where negation ends and where affirmation begins, and one cannot even be fully convinced that we are dealing first with the rationality of negation and later with that of affirmation.

Certainly, not all of the participants of this great scene that was ancient philosophy fully realized that the main intellectual battle was fought for the rationality of affirmation and the rationality of negation. According to Hegel, however, Sophists were aware of this, and even granted this opposition a higher rank than the sages mentioned here. In his presentation of their standpoint, he begins with a statement that "the notion that reason in the person of Anaxagoras recognized as the essence, is a simple negativity, in which all definiteness, everything that exists, and that which is separate melts. Nothing can avoid the concept. It is just an Absolute devoid of predicates, for which absolutely everything is merely a moment. There is nothing for it, so to speak, permanently fixed with rivets and nails." Never mind those "rivets and nails." What is most important here is the rational statement expressing affirmation, confirmation, and the "attachment" of something. A Sophist will certainly deny the existence of such rationality. This does not mean that with "the movement of Sophists," one cannot attach any rational affirmation. Hegel points out that those philosophers gave themselves the name of "teachers of wisdom." He also draws attention here to the fact that common sense many a time, also deliberately, "allows and even asserts the opposite to have a value also for consciousness; or it does not know that it says directly the opposite to what it means, its expression being thus only an expression of contradiction. Generally, in its actions, and not in its bad actions, ordinary understanding breaks there its maxims and its principles itself, and if it leads a rational life, it is properly speaking only a standing inconsistency, the making good of one narrow maxim of conduct through breaking off from others."[8] In short, even in sophistic affirmations, Hegel finds negations and all of this – in his opinion – is in a dialectical relationship.

---

[8] Cf. ibidem, p. 496 ff.

He also recalls that "it is particularly through the opposition to Socrates and Plato that the Sophists have come into such disrepute." Socrates is considered by him as the philosopher who, first, "launched the awareness of that what is, is mediated by thinking," second, "gave rise to moral philosophy" ("Socrates's teachings are basically morality"), and third, "brought morality philosophy from heaven to earth, to the homes and every-day life of men," but before he brought it there, "he had thoroughly thought through the contemporary philosophical speculation," and later, when he had already "brought it to earth," he "sealed" his truths on life with his own life. Hence, "he stands before us as one of those great plastic natures consistent through and through [...] resembling a perfect classical work of art which has brought itself to this itself to this height of perfection" as "a pious example of the moral virtues of wisdom, discretion, temperance, moderation, justice, courage inflexibility, firm sense of rectitude in relation to tyrants and people; he was equally removed from cupidity and despotism."

So far we have, in Hegel's presentation of Socrates, only affirmations and practically not even one negation. However, the latter appears already at the point when we learn from Hegel that this image of Socrates is a statue "hewn" by Plato and he starts "the procedure" of taking away this and that from Socrates's greatness or at least posing questions because, e.g. how is it possible that "no matter how much he drank" at night, in the morning he could hold forth a discussion (even "with a cup in his hand") with "Aristophanes and Agathon about comedy and tragedy." Certainly, there are more examples of such questions and as this dismantling of the Platonic monument progresses, Socrates takes on more and more human features. He does not cease to be a great master, but he is not a master at a level with the Greek gods, but on that of people walking the earth.

According to Hegel, it is in such a Socrates, living on earth, and experiencing both earthly joys and earthly pains, that we must seek the true source of his philosophy, including the rational affirmation and negation appearing in them and, of course, the dialectic relationship between them.[9] In the Hegelian sense, the Socratic dialectic is such a way ("method") of conducting a conversation so that: first, "everyone should be led to reflect on his own responsibilities" and, second, bring those with whom Socrates "entered into a discussion on their affairs [...] to think about that which is general," and that which is general is, or at least should be "in itself and for itself a valid truth, beauty."

This opens the gate for a Socratic dialectic of affirmation and negation. One of its most important aspects is what Hegel calls "Socratic irony," "a particular mode of carrying on intercourse between one person and another, and

---

[9] "His life and his philosophy are hewn from one block, this philosophizing is by no means retreating from the existence here and now into the free areas of pure thought." Ibidem, p. 554.

is thus only a subjective form of dialectic. It is for him a form of subjective dialectic, a way to keep in touch with the people [...]. What he wished to effect was, that when other people brought forward their principles, he, from each definite proposition [affirmation – remark – Z. D.], should deduce as its consequence the direct opposite of what the proposition stated (affirmation of an affirmation), or else allow the opposite (negation) to be deduced from their own inner consciousness without maintaining it directly against their statements (he does not negate that which they affirmed). [...] But as this opposite was a principle held by men as firmly as the other, he then went on to show that they contrasted themselves [that is, only a negation and an affirmation create a certain whole – Z. D.]. [...] Thus Socrates taught those with who he associated to know that they knew nothing; indeed, what is more, he himself said that he knew nothing." However, "not teaching, he taught," because "Socrates says that he does not know this or that, and inquires people about it; but to be more precise, such a sense is hidden in it that it is not known what this other imagines at the same time," and not only Socrates should find out, or some other philosopher using "Socratic irony," but also the one who imagines this something, and he should not only learn what he imagines, but also what is hidden behind these ideas and, according to each Socratic philosopher, behind them are some general, pre-approved "ultimate images, final sentences, which are known as something general, so that this knowledge is mutual."[10]

Let us make a note of one more attempt to draw the image of Socrates. It was done by Friedrich Nietzsche (1844-1900). He suggested that one should look at this philosopher through the eyes of his wife Xantippe, "the most insufferable woman ever living on earth." If one believed the ancient relations, Xantippe did everything so that her husband did not have any time to deal with his philosophical craftsmanship. At home she troubled him, and when he had had enough of it and wanted to meet his friends for a philosophical conversation, she was dissatisfied with it. Sometimes she poured a bucket of dirty water through the window straight onto his head and chased him and tore off his coat in the marketplace. His friends were indignant at this [...]. However, Socrates took all these outbursts with a philosophical peace. When he was given "a shower," he used to say beforehand: "Didn't I say that Xantippe's thunders end in rain." Nietzsche's answer to the question about what Xantippe achieved by constantly scolding her husband is that it was just the opposite effect to the one she desired, i.e. "the more she thundered forth at him, he even was the more inclined to practice his philosophical profession."[11]

---

[10] Cf. ibidem, p. 556 ff.

[11] Quoted after: W. Weischedel, *Die philosophische Hintertreppe. Die grossen Philosophen in Alltag und Denken*, Munich 1973, p. 29.

Was Xantippe's behaviour wise (rational)? To this simple question, unfortunately, one cannot provide a simple and unequivocal answer. This is because a lot depends on how this wisdom (rationality) is measured. If we assume that its measure or sign is the success of the action, Xantippe's behavior was unwise, and we can even say that it was stupid (irrational). But if one measures it by the standards of behavior and pro-social and asocial attitudes of that time, then the matter becomes complicated. In the light of these standards Socrates's and his companions' behavior had all the features of being antisocial. In fact, what were they doing? Actually, nothing – for days on end they wondered around the city and filled their time with philosophical disputes (read: "vain chatter"), and the greatest "loafer among those loafers" was Socrates, because "instead of taking care of his home, wife and sons, and performing his learned profession of stonemason, which he took over from his father, instead of introducing decent social changes, he engaged in wandering and in useless discussions with all the people."[12] The so-called "decent" Athenian obviously does not behave like that; and someone who behaves like that cannot count not only on social recognition, but must simply come to terms with serious repercussions from "respectable" Athenians (and such repercussions he encountered). Therefore, it seems that Socrates acted foolishly (irrationally), while Xantippe behaved wisely, as did the Athenian judges who tried him and sentenced him to death.[13]

By this I mean not only that Socratic philosophy can be interpreted and evaluated differently, but also that in it there can be found different rationalities, and some of them are complementary to one another, others are mutually exclusive, and still others complement and mutually exclude one another at the same time. It is also similar in the case of the philosophy of the Sophists, from which Socrates took over some of the proposals and oppositions including the way of this simultaneous complementarity and exclusion of

---

[12] "He likes finding coins in the street from time to time and this is his only contribution to the financing of his household in a commonly accepted manner; however, this is not the same as maintaining the family by honestly practicing one's craft. He can never afford to buy himself shoes; hence Aristophanes, author of comedies, presents him barefoot on the stage." Ibidem.

[13] This motif is also exposed by Plato in his *Apology of Socrates* – the apology of Socrates is obviously the defense of his wisdom (rationality), but it does not follow from the dialogue that there is no wisdom in the thinking and behavior of his accusers and judges. Certainly, it can be said that these are different wisdoms (rationalities), but still an explicit indication of their limits and "measures" is impossible; let somebody try to "decipher" to the end at least the fragment in which Socrates says: "For I, O Athenians I have acquired this character through nothing else than a certain wisdom. Of what kind, then, is this wisdom? Perhaps it is merely human wisdom. For in this, in truth, I appear to be wise. They probably, whom I have just now mentioned, possessed a wisdom more than human, otherwise I know not what to say about it; for I am not acquainted with it, and whosoever says I am, speaks falsely, and for the purpose of calumniating me." Cf. Plato, *The Apology of Socrates*, op. cit., p. 19 ff.

wisdom (rationality). The starting point here is the general assumption that a wise philosopher is one who can find the right measure of things and states of affairs, and apply it effectively in practice.

However, its direct complement is also the assumption that a philosopher is wise if he admittedly has not found such a measure, but has found such beacons (leads) of conduct that would allow him to navigate quite efficiently through this area of many unknowns that reality is. Although he does not achieve any of these values, the achievement of which is promised by the first one, he is convinced about which the other cannot be, i.e. that he does not take an appearance for reality; and even if he would make an error in something, he can withdraw in a relatively easy way to a secure position of standing aside and looking at what for a moment seemed to be the truth, good, justice, and yet another value. The first of these wisdoms belongs to the rationality of affirmation (statement/confirmation), while the other to the rationality of negation (doubt).

2. Plato

When idealizing Socrates, Plato idealized himself to some extent, i.e., he presented himself as that philosopher who, after covering the difficult road of posing rational questions and providing reasonable answers to them, gained such reasons that would tip any scale to his liking. However, whether it is a scale of confidence or that of uncertainty, he left the issue open enough that some people saw and still see him to be a skeptic rather than a dogmatist, while others saw him rather to be a dogmatist than a skeptic. This was already pointed out by Diogenes Laertius in his *Lives and Opinions of Eminent Philosophers*, when he wrote that "there is a great controversy about Plato whether he is or is not a dogmatist."[14] In modern times, a thesis has emerged and gained recognition of historians of philosophy that Plato's views evolved from dogmatism and skepticism.[15] Certainly, it facilitates to some extent the attempt to answer the

---

[14] "Dogmatizing is laying down dogmas, just as legislating is making laws. But the word dogma is used in two senses; to mean both that which we think, and opinion itself. Now of these, that which we think is the proposition, and opinion is the conception by which we entertain it in our minds. Plato then explains the opinions which ne entertains himself, and refutes false ones; and about doubtful matters he suspends his judgment. His opinions of matters as they appear to him he puts into the mouth of four persons, Socrates, Timaeus, an Athenian poet, and an Eleatic stranger." Cf. Diogenes Laertius, *Lives and Opinions...*, op. cit., p. 131 ff.

[15] "The concept of the "evolution" of the thought of Plato was introduced by Hermann in 1839, in a work that marks an important shift in Platonic studies [that is, *Geschichte und System der PlatonishenPhilosophie* – Z. D.] [...]. The thesis found exceptional agreement, and the conception

question of what the rationality of affirmation and negation looks like in Platonic philosophy.

To answer this question, I suggest starting with the statement of Diogenes Laertius who wrote that Plato, "considers wisdom as the knowledge of things which can be understood by the intellect, and which have a real existence: which has the Gods for its object, and the soul as unconnected with the body. He also, with a peculiarity of expression, calls wisdom also philosophy, which he explains as a desire for divine wisdom. But wisdom and experience are also used by him in their common acceptation; as, for instance, when he calls an artisan wise."[16] It follows that in Plato there is not one, but at least two types of rationality of affirmation, the first of which is oriented on that which is absolute and exclusively mental (spiritual), while the second is oriented on that which is relative and partly mental and partly sensual (corporal). The accuracy of this diagnosis is confirmed by historians of philosophy.[17] In Plato, these two types of rationality of affirmation are interrelated and hierarchized, and, in general, the main position is taken in his philosophy by a rationality oriented on that which is absolute and only mental, and, as we might call them, depending on the context, the rationality of the *Logos* (to Greek philosophers this term meant *argument*, *assessment*s, *measure*, *proposal*, *rule* and *reason*) or *Nous* (this term, in turn, meant *principle* and *intelligence,* among other things).

This rationality of affirmation, oriented on the absolute (absolute truth, absolute goodness, absolute justice, absolute beauty etc.), derives from that which is spiritual (rational) and leads to that which is spiritual (ideal). In his *Phaedo*, Plato postulated that the real causes (essences) should be reached, but "while we are in the body, and while the soul is mingled with the mass of evils, out desire will not be satisfied, and our desire is of the truth. For the body is

---

of *the evolution of Platonic thought* became an accepted rule of interpretation; also it received some important confirmations on the basis of the application of the method of stylistic analysis, statistical linguistics, and with the aid of the sophisticated methods of modern philology." Cf. G. Reale, *A History of Ancient Philosophy II: Plato and Aristotle*, Albany 1990, p. 26.

[16] Cf. Diogenes Laertius, *Lives and Opinions...*, op. cit., p. 135 ff.

[17] G. Reale interprets these two types of rationality of affirmation as the opposition of "myth" and "logos." The former, in Hegel, was presented as "contaminated by sensible forms" ("thus myth in Plato has a negative (philosophical) value"), whereas in Heidegger, it is "the most authentic expression of Platonic metaphysics," because "the logos, that is deployed in the theory if Ideas, is revealed as capable of stating *being*, but incapable of explaining *life*. Myth comes to its assistance in explaining life and, in a certain sense, overcomes logos and makes it mythology. Cf. G. Reale, *A History of Ancient Philosophy: Plato...*, op. cit., p. 30. T. Buksiński points to oppositions between Plato's *Logos* ("it is an expression of conceptual thinking: its dominance over the sensual image, over imagination, over myth") and *safrosine,* or *fronesis* ("this was an expression of prudence, or practical knowledge..."). Cf. T. Buksiński, *Dwa rozumy filozofii*, in: idem, *Rozumność i racjonalność*, Poznan 1997, p. 134 ff.

a source of endless trouble to us by reason of the mere requirement of food; and also is liable to diseases which overtake and impede us in the search after truth: and by filling us so full of loves, and lusts, and fears, and fancies, and idols, and every sort of folly, prevents our ever having, as people say, so much as a thought."[18]

In *Timaeus* he explains that this "foolery" and these "fancies" include "prophesying" – "the authors of our being, remembering the command of their father when he bade them create the human race as good as they could, that they might correct our inferior parts and make them to attain a measure of truth, placed in the liver the seat of divination. And herein is a proof that God has given the art of divination not to the wisdom, but to the foolishness of man. No man, when in his wits, attains prophetic truth and inspiration; but when he receives the inspired word, either his intelligence is enthralled in sleep, or he is demented by some distemper or possession. And he who would understand what he remembers to have been said, whether in a dream or when he was awake, by the prophetic and inspired nature, or would determine by reason the meaning of the apparitions which he has seen, and what indications they afford to this man or that, of past, present or future good and evil, must first recover his wits."[19] When one reaches the true causes in spite these things, "he attains to the purest knowledge of them who goes to each with the mind alone, not introducing or intruding in the act of thought sight or any other sense together with reason, but with the very light of the mind in her own clearness searches into the very truth of each; he who has got rid, as far as he can, of eyes and ears and, so to speak, of the whole body, these being in his opinion distracting elements which when they infect the soul hinder her from acquiring truth and knowledge."

In *Parmenides* he argued that these "true things" are a "class and an absolute essence" of everything, adding that "remarkable will be he who discovers all these things for himself, and having thoroughly investigated them is able to teach them to others."[20] And in *Cratylus*, while offering an answer to the question of how to recognize these "true things," he states that "things which are the same cannot change while they remain the same; and if they are always the same and in the same state, and never depart from their original form, they can never change or be moved."

In these statements there appears an attempt of bridging the gap between that which recognizes and that which is being recognized or which is the object of cognition. These "true things" appear to exist in the world of ideas. Plato

---

[18] Cf. Plato, *Phaedo*, in: *Plato's Apology, Crito and Phaedo*, Philadelphia 1897, p. 65 ff

[19] Cf. Plato, *Timaeus*, in: *Timaeus and Critias*, Digireads.com Publishing 2009, p. 50 ff.

[20] Cf. Plato, *Parmenides*, Teddington 2006, p. 30.

undertook the problem of the ontological status of these ideas (their being) in his different works and, in each case, he argued that these ideas ("incorporeal things") first, really exist; second, they are recognizable; third, they can only be known by reason; fourth, they must be known if we want to know "the real causes, i.e. the ultimate reasons" of that which constitutes results. According to G. Reale, the basic features of Platonic ideas are: "(a) *intelligibility* (the Idea is the quintessential object of the mind or intellect and graspable only by it); (b) *incorporeal* (the Idea belongs to a realm totally different from the sensible corporeal world); (c) *being in the full sense* (the Ideas are the beings that are really real); (d) *unchangeable* (the Ideas are devoid of any kind of change beside generation and corruption); (e) *self-identical* (the Ideas are in and of themselves; that is, absolutely objective); (f) *unities* (the Ideas are, each of them, a unity, unifying a multiplicity of things that participate them)."[21] In each of these points, rational affirmations appear. Without much effort, one can also see in them rational negations of various kinds, and that the cognitive status of the material world (sensory, physical, variable, etc.) is determined mainly by the oppositions (negations) to the world of ideas.[22] This is expressed in Plato in a kind of ontological and epistemological dualism, a dualism which translates into a series of complementary and mutually exclusive oppositions, such as the opposition of that which is ideal and that which is material, that which is mental and that which is sensual, that which constitutes true knowledge and that which is an opinion, etc.

In Platonic rationalism, it is important to articulate both these dualisms as well as to show how they can and should be transgressed – they should, because, according to Plato, everything that is manifested as multiplicity "refers" to some sort of unity, and the philosopher's task is to find unity in this multiplicity. In *The State* Plato says: "the one who can see the whole is a dialectician, while the one who cannot is not." It should be added that for

---

[21] Cf. G. Reale, *A History of Ancient Philosophy II: Plato...*, op. cit., p. 49.

[22] The basis for this distinction is Plato's separation of "that which always is" and "that which is always becoming" – "we must make a distinction and ask, What is that which always is and has no becoming; and what is that which is always becoming and never is? That which is apprehended by intelligence and reason is always in the same state; but that which is conceived by opinion with the help of sensation and without reason, is always in a process of becoming and perishing and never really is;" later, he adds: "Wherefore also we must acknowledge that there is one kind of being which is always the same, uncreated and indestructible, never receiving anything into itself from without, nor itself going out to any other, but invisible and imperceptible by any sense, and of which the contemplation is granted to intelligence only. And there is another nature of the same name with it, and like to it, perceived by sense, created, always in motion, becoming in place and again vanishing out of place, which is apprehended by opinion and sense." Cf. Plato, *Timaeus*, op. cit., p. 33 ff.

Plato, dialectics was the highest form of reason (rationality surpassing even such rationalized science as logic).[23] Logic, like arithmetic, geometry and astronomy, has the same "core" as dialectics; it is *Logos* manifested in different forms ("incarnations" and "shades" of meaning). Hence, Platonic dialectics can and should assume different forms. Plato wrote about its highest form, leading from that which constitutes multiplicity to that which constitutes unity, that is "a method of intelligent conversation" which "goes directly to the first principle and is the only science which does away with hypotheses in order to make her ground secure," and that "one is capable of wise conversation who closely attains a conception of the essence of each thing." This is a form of ascending dialectics, i.e. the one which applies the *synoptic* method. However, a dialectician is also the one who applies the *diairetic* (descending method); he starts from that which is the unity and arrives at different multiplicities. In the *Sophist,* Plato states that this dialectician "who can divide rightly, is able to see clearly one form (*idea*) pervading a scattered multitude, and many different forms contained under one higher form (*idea*); and again, one form (*idea*) knit together into a single whole and pervading many such wholes, and many forms, existing only in separation and isolation." Then, in *Philebus* he adds that "the one and many become identified by thought, and that now, as in time past they run about together, in and out of every word which is uttered, and that this union of them will never cease, and is not now beginning, but is, as I believe, an everlasting quality of thought itself, which never grows old;" however, it "must be accepted that some such unities really exist" and one must examine "how they exist, although each one of them is always one and the same, and can neither arise nor vanish. However, each one is still most strongly just this one unity."[24]

Thus, it can be said that, according to Plato, dialectical rationality is the rationality that is expressed not so much in non-equivocality or definiteness (as in logic) as in seeking and finding a center between that which is clear and that which is ambiguous, and then, between that which is variable and that which is permanent, and further, between that which is limited, and that which is unlimited, etc. In the final analysis, what is and what should be dialectical rationality is not prejudged by the human mind (even that of the wisest of wise men), but the reality in which we live and which we are trying to get to know. This reality seems to resemble a huge ball of threads of shimmering

---

[23] "[...] the latter being rather a theory of knowledge, discourse reasoning, theory of rational thought, dialectics is the art of applying logics in a discussion. [...] Logic is a static theory, whereas dialectics is a dynamic skill." Cf. K. Leśniak, *Platon*, Warsaw 1968, p. 54.

[24] Cf. Plato, *Philebus*, in: *Three Dialogues: Protagoras, Philebus, and Gorgias*, New York 2011, p. 59.

and different colours and shades, and the art of dialectical (rational) thinking can be reduced to finding in it the one that will enable us to go through this maze from the beginning to the end.

The extent of this bundle's entanglement and why it is entangled as it is, and not in any other way, is fully understood only by a mysterious God Demiurge. In *Timaeus*, Plato describes him as "A good Being" and even as "the best of intelligent beings," because it makes so that "all things should be good and nothing Bad, so far as this was attainable. Wherefore also finding the whole visible sphere not at rest, but moving in an irregular and disorderly fashion, out of disorder he brought order, considering that this was in every way better than the other. Now the deeds of the best could never be or have been other than the fairest, and the creator, reflecting on the things which are by nature visible, found that no unintelligent creature taken as a whole was fairer than the intelligent taken as a whole; and that intelligence could not be present in anything which was devoid of soul. For which reason, when he was framing the universe, he put intelligence in soul, and soul in body, that he might be the creator of a work which was by nature fairest and best."[25]

Minimalists seeking answers to the question about the meaning or the nature of divine creationism can already at this point feel satisfied, because what is most important in this regard has already been said. Yet Plato was not a minimalist but a maximalist and still had a lot to say both on this, as on many other important philosophical issues.

This is not the place to present the Platonic standpoint on all the problems he posed and solved. But it is worth drawing attention to the problem of the possibility of getting to know "the whole store of visible things." Plato seems to take this issue from two significantly different standpoints. In *Menon*, he inclines towards the thesis that this "store" is knowable – the justification for it is the belief that "the soul of man is immortal" and "as being immortal, and having been born again many times, and having seen all things that exist, whether in this world or in the world below, has knowledge of them all; and it is no wonder that she should be able to call to remembrance all that she ever knew about virtue, and about everything; for as all nature is akin, and the soul has learned all things, there is no difficulty in her eliciting or as men say learning, out of a single recollection all the rest, if a man is strenuous and does not faint."[26]

In *The Republic*, Plato evaluates and presents this possibility in a different way. To describe the cognitive situation of man, he quoted in this work the

---

[25] Cf. Plato, *Timaeus*, op. cit, p. 15 ff.
[26] Cf. Plato, *Meno*, Rockville 2009, p. 50.

metaphor of a cave. There he wrote: "Behold! Human beings living in an underground den, which has a mouth open towards the light and reaching all along the den; here they have been from their childhood, and have their legs and necks chained so that they cannot move, and can only see before them, being prevented by the chains turning round their heads. Above and behind them a fire is blazing at a distance... From above and from afar the light of the fire that burns behind them falls on them;" and he asks "how could they see anything but the shadows if they were never allowed to move their heads?"[27] Further, it appears that there is no way for them to know everything that casts the shadows; even if the one of them was freed from these shackles, then "he would not be able to see anything at all of what are now called realities." This metaphor is to show directly the unreliability of sensory cognition, and that while it implicitly argues for the fact that intellectual cognition is admittedly the only way to truth, following it does not mean that we shall manage to climb to the top of the hill on which truth seems to be. According to Plato, however, one should take the trouble to climb; "the journey upwards to be the ascent of the soul into the intellectual world of sight, according to my poor belief, which, at your desire, I have expressed – whether rightly or wrongly God knows. [...] my opinion is that in the world of knowledge the idea of good appears last of all, and is seen only with an effort; and, when seen, is also inferred to be the universal author of all things beautiful and right, parent of light and of the lord of light in this visible world, and the immediate source of reason and truth in the intellectual; and that this is the power upon which he who would act rationally either in the public or private life must have his eyes fixed."[28]

Undoubtedly, this is the Platonic creed – a confession of faith in human reason and human rationality, and also in the fact that it is necessary and worth making the effort to free oneself from the "shackles" of sensory illusion and climb to the top of rationality, however, without any guarantee, or even hope, that this effort will end with such an ultimate success which would be finding oneself on that perhaps real, and perhaps only mythical summit where "the idea of Good shines."

In Platonic terms, this faith has deep and diverse (not only epistemological) grounds; nevertheless, it is not able to acquire the qualities which logical or mathematical truths have. The latter are either such axioms themselves in view of which no one who understands the meaning of the expression "axiom" can and should raise any objections, or they logically result from such axioms. We can say about Plato from the time of his writing *Meno that* he was at least

---

[27] Cf. Plato, *The Republic*, New York 1991, p. 253 ff.
[28] Ibidem, p. 190.

inclined towards certain cognitive dogmatism. On the other hand, when writing *The Republic*, he did not so much cut himself off from it as he rather revealed both its rational and extra-rational foundations about such as faith and hope. Of course, both in the former and in the latter case we speak about the final reasons, but in the latter case, the concept of the *reason* should be considered – to use Plato's language – dialectically.

3. Aristotle

According to Diogenes Laertius, Aristotle (c. 384/83 – 322/21 BCE) "was the most eminent of all the pupils of Plato," but he "seceded from Plato while he was still alive" and founded the Lyceum in Athens ("the place suitable for walks") a peripatetic school (the term *peripatos* meant "strolling," in Greek). With his students he held discussions on various topics, as he saw the source of wisdom in *amazement* and *curiosity*, and it would be difficult to identify such areas of reality that did not arouse his curiosity. Thus, starting with Aristotle, it was assumed to treat philosophy not so much as *one* of the sciences, but as the science of sciences, while a philosopher was considered not so much as a specialist scholar, but rather as someone who is not an expert in anything but rather a person who managed to achieve such wisdom that allowed him to intelligently (rationally) speak on any topic and to offer wise counsel to all those who were not philosophers. Although this is intellectually suspicious, Aristotle still was able to explain and justify well enough, such that for many centuries philosophy was viewed as a kind of repository of wisdom, and he was seen as one of the wisest among the wise.[29]

Although Diogenes Laertius is not always a reliable source of information about the "lives and views" of those "famous philosophers" whose names appear on the pages of his work, often some information can be found that accurately points to the general line of thinking represented by those people. This is also so in the case of Aristotle. Diogenes Laertius wrote about this philosopher that from his point of view: "the philosophy of science is

---

[29] "His efforts were aimed, generally, at making philosophy validate itself as knowledge which is unconnected to any profit. Philosophy in itself should remain completely free and independent, but at the same time connected with praxis and creation. [...] This does not mean, however, that knowledge gained through philosophy cannot be useful in life. On the contrary, it becomes a necessary knowledge in order to lead a good life. [...] People who engage in philosophy come, through their activity, near to Gods (here Aristotle agreed with Plato), and achieve greatest happiness. However, they do not do it for themselves, but by sharing their knowledge with others, they allow them the opportunity of success in life." R. Elberfeld, *Was ist Philosophie...*, op. cit., p. 41 ff.

twofold, one practical and the other theoretical. The practical is divided into ethics and politics, and in the latter one there is talk about the country and the household; and the theoretical philosophy deals with physics and logic, but logic is not a separate branch, but it is the most effective tool for other branches of philosophy. And setting its two goals, he showed that which is likely and that which is true. For each of these purposes he used two means to help him, i.e. dialectics and rhetoric as well as analytics and philosophy in order to demonstrate what is true. He did not skip anything that relates to heuresis [...] or anything that relates to the court of law [...], or anything that relates to practical application." A little further, he added that "for the sole purpose he considered practicing virtues throughout the whole life," and that "virtue itself is not sufficient for happiness, one also needs bodily goods and external goods, because even a sage feels unhappy if he experiences suffering, privation and various deficiencies" and that "the virtues, however, do not go hand in hand; an intelligent and righteous man may at the same time be licentious and lacking self-control. A sage is not a man free of passions, but a man who controls his passions..."[30]

The sage that appears at the end of this statement or – which is just the same – "a wise and just man," argues that in Aristotle – as was in the case of his teacher, Plato – all this philosophizing, among other things, was meant to achieve maximum reason (rationality); but it seems that in this case, this rationality has been recognized as a necessary but not sufficient condition to achieve happiness, which is seen here as the main goal of all human activities. What else is, in Aristotle's opinion, needed to achieve this goal (apart from 'bodily and external goods'), and – of no less importance – how to achieve this goal, unfortunately, cannot be learned from Diogenes Laertius. This is because his presentation of the opinions of the philosopher is in fact extremely terse – if not even vague. Therefore, we must refer to the sources, i.e. to the writings of Aristotle.

The answers to the above questions are also influenced by those writings or groups of writings we begin with. It seems justified here to start from a group of his writings on morality – *Nicomachean Ethics,* not only because Aristotle considered the practice of virtue as the main goal of human life, but also because he said here that "human virtue is only the one in which activity of reason takes part" (which implies that there is no true morality without true rationality, and vice versa), and also he admitted that "life consisting in the activity of the reasonable element" is a characteristic distinguishing factor of man (which differentiates him both from the world of plants and that of animals), while

---

[30] Cf. Diogenes Laertius, *Lives and Opinions...*, op. cit., p. 181 ff.

performing this function by the soul was considered by him to be the highest of virtues accessible to man.[31] Here also Aristotle presented such a hierarchical division of virtues from which it appears that those are considered to be the highest that are connected with "the most noble part of the soul," i.e., with reason (they are the so-called dianoetic virtues, one of which is wisdom). He also pointed here to the existence of "the less noble part of the soul," and to its internal differentiation, which means that "the element without reason seems itself to have two parts. For the vegetative part has no share at all in reason, while the part consisting in appetite and desire in general does share in it in a way, in so far as it listens to and obeys it." Certainly, human thinking and behavior is the more intelligent the better those notions "of the appetites and of desire" are controlled and disciplined by reason.

It must also be noted that in this work there are both the distinction of different types of wisdom (rationality) as well as an indication of its highest kind "wisdom in arts." He observes here – "Wisdom in skills we attribute to their most exacting practitioners; for example, we call Pheidias a wise sculptor and Polycleitus a wise maker of statues, meaning nothing by wisdom other than virtue in a skill. But some people we think are wise in general, not in some particular sphere or wise in any other respect [...] so the wise person must not only know what follows from the first principles of a science, but also have a true understanding of those first principles."

Aristotle's answer to the question of how to achieve this understanding amounts to saying that one should learn and practice the virtues, but practicing them means contributing to the better and better mastery of them: "men come to be builders, for instance, by building; harp-players, by playing on the harp: exactly so, by doing just actions we come to be just; by doing the actions of self-mastery we come to be perfected in self-mastery; and by doing brave actions brave." All the virtues listed here require the support of reason, but moderation – also known as "the right means" – is one of them which determines the others. In *Ethics* [Magna Moralia], he explains that moderation "is a mean state, having for its object-matter Pleasures, [and] the state of utter absence of self-control has plainly the same object-matter."[32] This means that

---

[31] "[If] we take the characteristic activity of a human being to be a certain kind of life; and if we take this kind of life to be activity of the soul and actions in accordance with reason, and the characteristic activity of the good (virtuous) person to be to carry this out well and nobly, and a characteristic activity to be accomplished well when it is accomplished in accordance with the appropriate virtue; then if this is so, the human good turns out to be activity of the soul in accordance with virtue, and if there are several virtues, in accordance with the best and most complete." Aristotle, *Nicomachean Ethics*, Cambridge 2000, p. 12.

[32] Aristotle, *Ethics*, Pennsylvania 2004, p. 76.

you cannot be brave without being moderate, because the first one turns out to be "the proper middle" between impudence and cowardice. Later, he explains that without mastering and practicing this virtue one cannot learn and practice many other virtues, e.g. gentleness (it is "the right middle" between quick temper and insensitivity), munificence (it is the middle between extravagance and miserliness), friendship (a middle between flattery and hostility), dignity (a middle between servility and conceit), magnanimity (a middle between vanity and pusillanimity), or generosity (the middle between prodigality and parsimony).

Already at this point we can make an attempt at outlining the general image of a wise man (a sage). To be sure, this is a person oriented in his thinking and action not on solving great problems of metaphysics (such as the beginning and the end of the world, or whether order or disorder prevails in it), but on solving the fundamental problems of man's existence, especially the moral issues without the solution of which he cannot achieve what he mostly desires. It turns out that everyone – even a sage – wants to achieve happiness, and he wants to achieve this not in some other world, but in this world, in which he faces the hardships of daily life ("the sufferings, privations and various shortcomings"). It is also someone who had admittedly already found a way of reaching this goal (it is by going "in the middle of the road"), yet he is aware that this undertaking is not easy; even if he is already on this way, he must be aware of the propensity to "walk their separate ways" of those parts of the soul which in their nature are neither rational nor submit easily to the control of reason. This is largely someone independent, in his thinking and actions, of other people's judgments, opinions and evaluations, or – what is just the same – he has a deep inner conviction that if his own mind will not help him, then no one else and nothing will help him. But when answering the question: Where does he take this conviction and all his other wisdom from, he will not maintain that this is solely the result of his own thoughts and life experiences. On the contrary, he will argue that, at least when it comes to general guidelines, it is worth listening to wise men (philosophers), i.e., those who sacrificed their lives wooing this *Sophia* (Wisdom), which is so mysterious to many, and who managed to get to know more than one of its secrets. In many concrete problems of everyday life, however, one can count solely on one's mind, and more specifically on one's common sense (*phrónesis*) – in his *Nicomachean Ethics*, Aristotle defines it as "a permanent disposition to act based on a correct consideration of what is good or what is bad for man" and situated it among the dianoethical virtues, i.e. the ones which belong to "the most notable part of the soul."

The wisdom of these sages is something much more than wisdom based on common sense. An answer to the question of what it is and should be, can be found in Aristotle's *Organon*, i.e., in his writings on logic and epistemology. In fact it is there where Aristotle argues that this wise man is, more than anything else, an "analyst" (he used this term to describe a logician), i.e., someone who "achieves knowledge through a proof": "By knowledge I mean a syllogism creating scientific knowledge" and "syllogism is a statement in which when something is assumed, something else must result than that which was assumed because it was assumed" and a syllogism can be "perfect" (then "if one does not need anything more than that which was assumed"), or "imperfect" (then "if one needs for it one or more sentences, which although necessary due to adopted terms, however, are not accepted because of the premises)."[33]

This sage is also someone who can unequivocally define basic concepts, i.e. either to define them (according to Aristotle, a definition is "a discourse which expresses the essence," or "a discourse which expresses the nature of things," or a discourse which expresses the substance of things"), or to indicate the reasons why they cannot and need not be defined (one cannot define categories, because these are the most general concepts, among others, used to define other concepts), and, further, he can accurately indicate the number of such concepts that cannot be defined (according to Aristotle, there are ten and only ten of them), while still further, he is able to conduct a logical and grammatical analysis of sentences (Aristotle calls this "hermeneutics"). Certainly, there are more of these "furthers," because the wise man turns out to be not only an effective logician but also a not less able mathematician, physicist, metaphysician and rhetorician. In each of these sciences and arts (according to Aristotle, rhetoric is an art – "undoubtedly a useful art" since "it is adding to truth and justice more than to their opposites") as well as in many other areas (such as, e.g. poetics or politics) this sage in a masterly manner uses his intellect and those abilities that support him, and he can overcome and exercise control over those who oppose him so that they are not an obstacle in attaining happiness.

It is not possible to give a clear-cut answer to the question whether this wise man uses one and the same reason in all of this, or whether at one time he uses one reason, and at another time a different kind of reason. It cannot

---

[33] Cf. Aristotle, *The Works of Aristotle: Organon or Logical Treatises of Aristotle*, New York 2001, p. 40 ff. According to G. Reale, "Aristotelian logic has [...] a determinable philosophical origin, it marks the moment in which the philosophical logos, until then completely matured through the structuring of all its problems in the manner which we have seem, becomes capable of stating the problem about its own status and has a precise way of proceeding; and thus, after having learned to reason, the logos succeeds in establishing what the nature of reason is itself, viz., what it is to reason, how much, and on what is it possible to reason." Cf. G. Reale, *A History of Ancient Philosophy II: Plato...*, op. cit., p. 351.

be ruled out that Aristotle assumed that man has various kinds of reasons and uses them depending on particular needs and circumstances.[34] However, it cannot be ruled out either that he assumed the existence of only one human reason – the one that is the subject to changes depending on the level of his education and on the functions he performed. Under this assumption, a mathematical mind would be a lower form of development of the ability of the human soul than logical reason, but both would be a higher form of development than practical reason.

In turn, in the case of the latter, a higher value should be placed in that part of reason which can be applied in the so called productive sciences (also called "arts" by Aristotle) than the one which reveals its presence in everyday life and prosaic activities. What hangs in the balance here is also the possibility of such a distinction which would place on one side reason conceived as the capacity for abstract (conceptual) thinking, while one the other side reason understood as the capacity for activities which enable man to achieve his goals in practical life. In any case, in Aristotle, reason and rationality are once treated substantially (emphasizing the essentiality of rationality) and, at other times, functionally (focusing on the implementation of specific tasks by the reason).

Postscript

For the determination of the Aristotelian standards of rationality in philosophical tradition it is essential to answer the question about the relationship of Aristotle's philosophy to that of Plato, i.e., to answer the question whether generally, in the latter, the negation or affirmation prevails or not. It has long been the subject of bitter controversy. But according to some authors (e.g. Diogenes Laertius) Aristotle essentially broke off from the teachings of his master and teacher. However, there was no shortage of those who saw and still see more important convergences than divergences between these two philosophies. Such a view was preached by Plotinus (203-269 CE) who, in his *Enneads*, tried to show above all the philosophical greatness of Plato, but who also has a lot of good to say about Aristotle, even if he points out some of his errors and ambiguities; indeed, he also says that these errors are relatively easy to correct, while the ambiguities can be clarified by referring to Plato's work.[35]

---

[34] According to T. Buksiński, Aristotle displays "the following types of reason (its functions, or states): passive, active, potential, present, dianoetic, noetic, and also scientific and philosophical." Cf. T. Buksiński, *Dwa rozumy filozofii*, op. cit., p. 142 ff.

[35] For example, in Aristotle, "Time [is] being called a measure of Movement when it should have been described as something measured by Movement and then defined in

The proximity of Plato's philosophy to that of Aristotle was also emphasized by St. Augustine – in his philosophical dialogue *Contra Academicos* he wrote that "Aristotle and Plato agree with each other (although they did so in such a way that to the unskilled and inattentive they seemed to disagree)." Later, opinions on this proximity between Aristotle and Plato were more mixed.[36] In the Middle Ages, Arabic tradition put the two philosophers together. In Christian philosophy, however, opting for one or the other often meant finding oneself on one of the sides of an intellectual barricade, being either in the significantly different rationalistic options, or even, on the one hand, within rationalism, and on the other, within any of the instances of irrationalism of the time.[37]

An important voice in the discussion on this topic is that of Giovanni Reale, who proposed a metaphor of "the first and second voyage" of ancient philosophers. In its light, both philosophers are situated in "the second voyage," or "when the journey is interrupted by the absence of wind, and the journey continues using the oars." "The 'first voyage' made with the wind in the sails would correspond, hence, to that followed completely by the Naturalists and their method; the second voyage made with the oar, and hence very tiring and difficult, corresponds to a new type of method, that leads to the conquest of the sphere of the supersensible. The wind in the sails of the Physicists were the senses and sensations, the oars of the second voyage are reasonings and hypotheses; and the new method is based on these."[38] Of course, these oars were used both by Plato and Aristotle. The latter's belonging to this group of "sailors" of "the Second voyage" is pointed out by the recognition of "the existence of a supersensible and transcendent reality." The main difference between Plato and Aristotle in this matter would amount to the fact that Ar-

---

its essential nature [...]; Plato does not make the essence of Time consist in its being either a measure or a thing measured by something else." Cf. Plotinus, *Six Enneads*, Whitefish 2004, p. 278.

[36] A little further, he adds: "[True philosophy] has finally emerged after many centuries and many controversies. [...] This philosophy is of this world [...] but of the other world, the intelligible world." Cf. St. Augustine, *Against the academicians and The Teacher*, Indianapolis 1995, p. 91.

[37] This is shown by, for example, Jan Legowicz in his presentation of the philosophy of the Middle Ages. Cf. J. Legowicz, *Zarys historii filozofii*, Warsaw 1967, p. 164 ff.

[38] Cf. G. Reale, *A History of Ancient Philosophy II: Plato...*, op. cit., p. 39. Interestingly, among the most prominent "helmsmen" of the "first voyage" Reale places Anaxagoras (500-428 BCE); Plato "departed" from him not because he did not agree with the ordering role of the mind, but because since Anaxagoras maintained the thesis of ordering mind, he "ought to have explained the criterion of the best in function of what it does; and on the basis of this criterion he must explain the conditions; [...] but Anaxagoras does not do this. He introduces the Mind, but he does not attribute any role to it as just indicated; but he continues to assign the role of cause to the *physical elements* (air, aither, water, etc.)." Ibidem, p. 38.

istotle replaced "the Platonic concept of the supersensible understood as an intelligible reality" with "the conception of supersensible usually understood as the Intellects;" these prove to be: "a. God, the immovable Mover, b. beings similar to the First Mover, c. beings that are hierarchically structured, d. rational souls existing in men."[39] From this confrontation emerges a picture of Aristotle as a philosopher "who tends to more coherence and cohesion than Plato did," but above all, a great metaphysician and a Platonic metaphysician also, and, in any case, the one who "maintained the Platonic theorem of the metaphysical primacy of form," and the one who also preserved the Platonic "fundamental eidetic conception."

Of course, there are some similarities between the philosophical standards of rationality proposed by Plato and Aristotle. However, there are also significant differences between them and these differences ultimately constitute themselves as different types of rationality. Among others, there are convergences and divergences in their understanding of the theoretical and practical possibilities of reason, which is the best "sentient," and the one that finds itself in the world of speculation and theory, i.e. that of ideas, axioms, theorems and postulates. Indeed, in Aristotle, such reason also appears, but it appears not only to demonstrate its ability of speculative and exact thinking (and it shows itself, among other things, in metaphysics and logic), but also to show its willingness to resolve all human problems. Although it appears that they cannot be easily and quickly resolved, and perhaps such a venture will never end with a definite success, still this reason finds the need, possibility and capability of admitting to his limitations, and which is no less important – he can point out the limitations of those with whom he must interact in various stages of gaining still greater efficiency (rationality), and to justify the alliances and compromises concluded; this justification shows how huge, diverse and full of numerous pitfalls is the area in which he is forced to move. All this would amount to a skeptical contestation, if he did not have a rational plan to overcome these difficulties and a strong determination and firm faith that they can and must be overcome. But he has it and teaches it (in his ethics) like a catalogue of virtues that must be implemented (if a man wants to be somehow different from plants) – step by step, gradually climbing to higher and higher levels of rationality.

At one of the initial stages of moving toward the greatest intellect, he finds an ally in common sense; he uses it not because he has great confidence in it (because he does not), but because he is sufficiently familiar with his "craft" – like a builder who already has a plan of a house, but lacks experience and skills

---

[39] Cf. ibidem, p. 392.

to erect it by himself, and therefore must be assisted by the one who indeed does not provide any intellectual support, but rather helps him avoid the most serious errors. In a sense, this is an answer to the question of Aristotle's attitude towards the Sophists; he did not negate their commonsense wisdom, but he treated it as ancillary and as a wisdom which requires control and corrections on the part of the intellect.

Anyway, Aristotle firmly believed that every person is equipped with some kind of reason and has the ability to achieve an ever greater rationality through developing the efficiency of his mind, and through experience; this is one of the conditions not only for forming rational alliances but also dissolving them if they cease to be useful, and to start searching for new and more useful allies. On the question of whether at some point this reason appears strong enough to suffice by itself, Aristotle does not give an unequivocal answer. However, in my opinion, there is no such argumentation which could justify the rationality of such expectations. This means that the Aristotelian reason (taken in its "noblest" element) in fact cannot become what it becomes in the interpretation of Giovanni Reale, i.e. God, the First Mover, or "a being similar to the First Mover." It cannot become this *Logos* written with a capital letter, i.e., a being which is completely rational in itself and which introduces rationality and its derivatives (such as harmony or order) to everything that really exists. However, it can and, in Aristotle's opinion, should become the *logos* written with a small letter, i.e., the chief virtue, principle and measure of human thinking and practical action.

Perhaps he could also become a *mythologos*, i.e. someone from the realm of the parable about demi-gods and heroes, and faith in the possibility and need of existence of various forms of heroism and bravery – but not without significant reservations; the fundamental question is whether he is capable of exercising reasonable control of this faith and, above all, if he does not confuse it with what constitutes its intellectual background; let me remind that, among other things, this is the Aristotelian "organon," using strong reasons, logical evidence and strict concepts. Yet I will not try to answer the question whether, having such a background of the Greek *mýthos* (being, after all, closer to legend and parable than to knowledge or truth), there is still something significant enough to grant it – even if conditionally – "full citizenship" in the so called high intellectual culture.

Chapter II

Renaissance traditions

1. Nicholas of Cusa

Historians generally agree that Nicholas of Cusa (1401-1464), as a thinker, was, in more than one respect, towering over other Renaissance philosophers. According to Paul Oskar Kristeller, he was "the most original and profound" mind that appeared in the fifteenth century.[1] However, Etienne Gilson in his *History of Christian Philosophy in the Middle Ages*, does not consider him as a Renaissance scholar, but rather as one who belongs to the decadent Middle Ages, and places him among those who defined and marked the last stage in that great intellectual journey which was the theology and philosophy of the Middle Ages.[2] In the chapter titled *Journey's End,* he concludes that Cusanus was "a great figure, towering over his age", and his work *On Learned Ignorance* "an intimate blending of theology and philosophy in which it is almost impossible to draw any dividing line between them other than in words. Moreover, it is a philosophical synthesis spontaneously adapted to the needs of its own times." Although I would not be inclined to agree with each of these statements, I do agree with the thesis that Cusanus's work mentioned here is evidence

---

[1] Kriestler places him among the three most prominent Platonists of the fifteenth century, the other two being Marsilio Ficino and Giovanni Pico Della Mirandola. "Although Cusanus, Ficino, and Pico – he writes – were not pure Platonists, they were deeply infused with Platonism, and their works, similarly to those of Plato and Neo-Platonists, were circulated until the end of the fifteenth century, and in the sixteenth century gained great popularity both in manuscript and in print..." Cf. P. O. Kristeller, *Renesans w historii myśli filozoficznej*, in: idem, *Humanizm i filozofia*, Warsaw 1985, p. 175 ff.

[2] Cf. E. Gilson, *History of Christian Philosophy in the Middle Ages*, London 1980.

of profound changes that occurred in the thought of the most independent minds of that era.

Its protagonist is not – as one might judge by the title – a man, but God. The intellectual battle presented in *On Learned Ignorance*, however, is fought here by an intellectual who uses his mind, and the battle is fought for his utmost intellectual proximity to God, which he eventually achieves (at least in Cusanus's opinion). In this way the second most important hero of this battle emerges. Certainly, he is not as perfect as God, but still, without his intellect, no one living here and now would ever know of either divine perfection or of one's own weakness. This definition and self-definition through a confrontation of perfection with imperfection, as well as taking advantage of the opportunities provided by affirmation and negation is present in all three books which make up the treatise. In the last book it is raised to the rank of a negative but rational theology. This is the final point at which Cusanus arrives in this treatise.

At the starting point he is not so much a rationalist-theologian, but rather a rationalist philosopher. First, he presents a certain sequence of logically related principles, arguments and conclusions of varying degrees of generality. In their light everything that is, is "by the gift of God," and everything "by the gift of God" has "a natural desire to exist in the best manner." This tendency is shown by everything that "we see in all things," and "we see" that everything "[acts] towards this end" and "we have instruments adapted thereto." To the question: what are these instruments, he answers that these include "a sound, free intellect" which "desires to attain unto the true through scrutinizing all things." To the question of what happens to that intellect when it is "unsound" (due to, for example, sickness)?, he replied that it "misleads." To the question "What is most true?", he replies that it is "that from which no sound mind can withhold assent". It is clear that the "unsound mind" contradicts "the truest of truths", and this is a sign of its sickness.[3]

These and other statements appear in the first paragraph of Chapter I of the first book of this treatise. Its title, *How it is that knowing is not-knowing*, expresses one of the main rules of the Cusanian method of inquiry into truth – it says that "every inquiry is comparative and uses the means of comparative relation" and that complex "comparative relations" should be reduced to simpler ones, because when they become simpler, "judgment easily apprehends [it]," and once it properly captures it, it becomes certain. And no longer is there anything "further," because what a sound mind means is certainty, including confidence in what one can know, and what one cannot know. Certainly, all this is also philosophy, to be more precise, the rational philosophy of learning

---

[3] Cf. Nicholas of Cusa, *On Learned Ignorance*, Minneapolis 1985, p. 5.

and cognition. Cusanus tries to convince us about it, among other things, by including a list of those authorities to whom he refers in this short chapter, but which is densely "woven" with philosophical ideas, assumptions and postulates. Among others, he refers to such figures as Pythagoras, Socrates and Aristotle. There are no references to theologians.

There are no theologians mentioned in Chapter II of this book either. Instead, an issue appears that may well belong both to philosophy and theology, that of "the Absolute Maximality." All the considerations found in this chapter clearly go in the direction of the philosophy of being, more precisely, the Absolute Being, understood in the way found in Aristotelian metaphysics.

Cusanus says there that the "Absolute Maximality is Absolute Being, through which all things are that which they are, so from Absolute Being there exists a universal oneness of being which is spoken of as "a maximum deriving from the Absolute [Maximum]" – existing from it contractedly and as a universe. This maximum's oneness is contracted in plurality, and cannot exist without plurality."

This general statement is followed by details provided for mainly either justifying or explaining reasons such as, e.g., "the universe exists-in-plurality only contractedly, we shall seek among the many things the one maximum in which the universe actually exists most greatly and most perfectly as in its goal the existence of the Universe in plurality is possible only via contraction, in that plurality we single out one thing, the largest one in which the Universe currently exists the most perfectly and most fully as in its purpose," etc. Another noteworthy Cusanian statement is that the aim of the disentangling of all these reasons is "to leave behind perceptible things, so that the reader may readily ascend unto simple intellectuality." No matter how interpreted, it will always turn out that the author of this treatise does not mean the sensory cognition, but a mental one, especially the one in which intellectual "judgment apprehends, captures things." Of course, one "easily apprehends" that which is simple itself or in itself or manifests itself as simple, or it is complex, but it can be broken down into simple elements.

The chapter that follows is titled: *The precise truth is incomprehensible*. It is incomprehensible because "there is no comparative relation of the infinite to the finite;" "The Maximum is infinite;" and "therefore, it is not the case that by means of likenesses a finite intellect can precisely attain the truth about things. [...] Hence, the intellect [...] never comprehends truth so precisely." However, it can and should (if it is "sound" and its needs are "sound") capture the boundaries of mental cognitive abilities ("intellect may be likened unto possibility"), or – which is just the same – "to possess a learned understanding of their ignorance," and where the "more deeply we are instructed in this ignorance, the closer we approach to truth," the more we shall be "enlightened," or the more "we come closer to truth." To recapitulate, in the confrontation with the "Maximum," human intellect has to recognize and does in fact recognize (if it is sound) its limitations, or simply its inability to know the "Maximum," regardless of whether it is a vague and unidentifiable "Absolute Maximum," or some very distant contradictions, or a God that is determined, or at least determined in some way by theologians. However, this same intellect can (and should) be understood not only by its inability to reach the "Absolute Maximum," but also its power – expressed, among others, in that it quite clearly understands that "the Absolute Maximum incomprehensibly understandable" and that "the Maximum is One" and "Absolute Oneness, to which nothing is opposed, is Absolute Maximality, which is the Blessed God," praised not only by those of deep faith (such as "our most holy teachers" in favour of the Trinity), but also by men of profound thought – such as Pythagoras (stating that "One is a trine"), or "the divine Plato, who [...] says in the *Phaedo* that as it exists in itself, there is one Form or Idea of all things." Of course, there are many more such references to specific individuals and their ideas in Book I of this treatise. They have to lead the reader to believing that the ways of rational philosophy and rational theology do not diverge, but rather converge, provided that, obviously, the driving and the steering force in them is the human intellect; the same one of which mathematicians and logicians made and still make use (in this book there are quite numerous references to the achievements of the former).

In the last chapters of his book (Chapters XXIV to XXVI), Cusanus puts into question the rationality of affirmative theology and points to the arguments in favour of the adoption of negative theology. In both cases the reference is to "the First Maximum" (God). Against affirmative theology this is that "the affirmative names we ascribe to God befit Him [only] infinitesimally. For such [names] are ascribed to Him in accordance with something found in created things."[4] The evidence of its slim rationality is demonstrated by the fact that "the pagans likewise named God from His various relationships to created things." On the other hand, what certainly speaks in favour of negative theology is the whole of "learned ignorance," i.e., everything that was in the treatise previously agreed upon and stated, in particular the general thesis that God is "infinitely greater than all nameable things above anything that can be called," but to be called it must be recognized. "It is clear that in theological matters negations are true and affirmations are inadequate, and that, nonethe-

---

[4] "Therefore, since any such particular or discrete thing, or thing having an opposite, can befit God only very minutely: affirmations are scarcely fitting [...]." Ibidem, p. 41.

less, the negations which remove the more imperfect things from the most Perfect are truer than the others."

It must be clearly stated that Cusanus does not negate the value of positive theology completely. However, he acknowledges it to be less rational than negative theology, and situates it at the level of those cults, which, although they "ascend to God," are in this ascent, to a greater extent, reliant on faith rather than intellect. The answer to the question what kind of intellect they rely on is simple and obvious – they especially rely on that which is represented by Cusanus, and on the intellect of those whom he considers to be philosophical and theological authorities.[5]

Book II of this treatise is a presentation of Cusanian metaphysics (in the sense of the term at the time), i.e., "[inquiring] a bit more about those things which are all-that-which-they-are from the Absolute Maximum." The author assures that this going into detail "will be very advantageous to [...] our instruction in ignorance," which – taken literally – means as much as that this metaphysics is rational and it is an extension of the previously presented elements of rational epistemology and theology. And indeed they were cited very briefly in Chapter I of the book – not only to be fixed in mind, but also to indicate those oppositions which, on the basis of Cusanian rationalism are of a fundamental character – such as sensual-rational (or intellectual), finite-infinite, relative-absolute, plurality-unity, etc. They are intended to be pairs of opposites, which are logically and ontically complementary and at the same time mutually exclusive. "Let me say, still making inferences from the same basis: Since with regard to opposites [...] we also find degrees of comparative greatness, we do not come to the pure oppositeness of the opposites – i.e., to that wherein they agree precisely and equally." However, on this basis "we pursue the knowledge of things rationally, so that we may know that, in one thing, composition is present in a certain simplicity and in another thing simplicity is present in composition, [that] in one thing corruptibility [is present] in incor-

---

[5] "The critical edition of his *Learned Ignorance* abounds in references to Thierry of Chartres, to Gilbert of la Porrée, to Clarenbaud of Arras, John of Salisbury and others whose inspiration was akin to his own doctrine. Nicholas went still farther back into the past, to the sources of these latter sources: Chalcidius, Macrobius, Asclepius, Hermes Trismegistus are all well known to him, and since the Platonism of these authors was in line with the doctrine of Denis the Aeropagite, Nicholas could not doubt in their legitimacy." E. Gilson, *History of Christian philosophy...*, op. cit., p. 540. The last of the authorities of Nicholas listed above (also known by the name of Pseudo-Dionysius the Areopagite, was the author of such treatises as: *On the Divine Names, Mystical Theology, On the Ecclesiastical Hierarchy, On the Celestial Hierarchy*; the system of philosophy and theology he outlined in these works is called "dialectical theology" or "negative theology" (one of its main theses is that a reference to the Divine allows producing a rational contradiction to every rational assumption). For more on this topic see: T. Whittaker, *The Neo-Platonists*, London 1928.

ruptibility" etc. For someone who absorbed the Socratic-Platonic dialectics (and surely, Cusanus did), this should be easily understood.

Therefore, answering the question: "what does the Sacred Ignorance tell us about being" (here "ignorance" must be considered dialectically), he states that it teaches that: 1. "[a] created being derives from the being of the First in a way that is not understandable," "nothing exists from itself except the unqualifiedly Maximum (in which *from itself, in itself, through itself* and *with respect to* itself are the same thing [...]);[6] 2. "In a way that cannot be understood the Maximum enfolds and unfolds all things", i.e. (and here appears the unfolding of this "folded" thought), how "rest is oneness which enfolds motion," "motion is the unfolding of rest," "the past and the future are the unfolding of the present," and "the present is the enfolding of all present times," etc.; 3. "The universe, which is only a contracted maximum, is a likeness of the Absolute;" and in this way "the world, or universe, is a contracted maximum and a contracted one" and the Maximum is "simple Oneness" etc.

Let us take a brief look only at the first four chapters of this book. The whole work consists of thirteen chapters, and each is supposed to enlighten our ignorance about the Being and beings, in general, and in great detail. It is worth noting that in the last of them (*The admirable divine art in the creation of the world and of the elements*), there is a reference not only to God who has given man "a face which is turned toward Him and a consuming desire to seek [Him]," but also to those who have this face and are not only able to admire "the size, beauty, and order" of the world, but also can know and speak about this work of God – either "through Arithmetic," or "through Logic," or "using the Dialectic" (Cusanus himself writes only the word "arithmetic" using a capital letter), and in any case, using the intellect. Without the intellect we would perhaps be "stunned by the artistry and perfection of God" but there would be neither any of these teachings, nor any other such science or art that would enable us to identify and properly evaluate this "artistry and perfection."

"Having set forth the few preceding points about how the universe exists in contraction, I will very briefly expound for Your most admirable Diligence the concept of Jesus. [I will do so] to the end that – as regards Him who is both Absolute Maximum and contracted Maximum." This entire sentence of the *Preface* to the third book of this work could have disturbed the Church censors of his time because, for example, why "to the end," and what does it mean "contracted maximum"? Cusanus was, however, not afraid of such questions. In fact, he assumed that this dissertation would reach the people using reason and would defend itself by force of the rational arguments presented in it.

---

[6] The first part of this statement is the title of Chapter II; the second part appears in the first sentence of the chapter.

And so, he first gives a brief reminder of what was said in Book I (which is most important, from the viewpoint of Cusanian rationalism), then he also writes briefly about the "contracted beings" and about "contraction" and the Universe (e.g., that "exhaust the infinite, absolute maximum power of God"), and a little more extensively about God (e.g., that he is "the Beginning, the Middle and the End of the universe and of each thing"). Generally, in these reminders and repetitions there is nothing which has not been said by Christian theologians throughout the centuries.

Of course, Cusanus was also a theologian. He was a theologian, but a theologian of a new type, i.e., one who referred to the great tradition of philosophical rationalism. Therefore, he argued in subsequent chapters of this part of *On Learned Ignorance* that "the maximum which is contracted to this, or that, and that which there cannot be greater, cannot exist without the Absolute [Maximum]," that "the maximum contracted [to a species] also the Absolute [Maximum; it is both]", that "only in the case of the nature of humanity can there be such a maximum [individual]" etc.; up to a short chapter titled *The Church* which, if it is to be the true Church, must be a union of the faithful – with union in faith and love, but also in rationality, or at least in its pursuit since "Blessed is God, who has given us an intellect which cannot be filled in the course of time." "This is the church of the triumphant" (I will add: "the triumphant intellectuals," A/N). "Here the true man Christ Jesus is united, in supreme union, with the Son of God – in so great a union that the humanity exists only in the divinity; it is present in the divinity by means of an ineffable hypostatic union – [present] in such a way that it cannot be more highly and more simply united if the truth [i.e., the reality] of the nature of the humanity is to remain. Then every *rational* nature (emphasis – A/N), – provided that in this life it turn to Christ with supreme faith, hope and love – is united with Christ the Lord."[7] Undoubtedly, this is a kind of confession of faith – faith in Jesus Christ, but also faith in human reason (intellect). And the intellect, if fully utilized, can and should support the belief in Christ.

2. Erasmus of Rotterdam

Erasmus of Rotterdam (1469-1536) was, in many respects, an exceptional fig-ure. By experts on the Renaissance, he is recognized as an innovator, or at least as a thinker that announced the coming of a new age. Jacob Burckhardt places him among those great scholars who, in the sixteenth century, took over the torch of wisdom of the Greek and Italian humanist scholars of the fourteenth

---

[7] Cf. ibidem, p. 148.

and fifteenth century.[8] Johan Huizinga, in contrast, sees in Erasmian thought a reference to the characteristic elements of the intellectual culture of the period of optimism and affirmation of life.[9] Panajotis Kondylis placed Erasmus among those thinkers whose doubtful thinking prepared the grounds for the birth of the Enlightenment, tearing down the pillars of medieval intellectual culture, such as Christian theology and the related scholastic logic, ethics, and anthropology.[10] These opinions are quite accurate.

In the thematically diverse literary achievements of Erasmus, a particularly significant place is occupied by his *Praise of Folly*. His youthful *Colloquies* (*Colloquia familiar*) were a kind of a trial run to writing the aforementioned dissertation.[11] This collection of *Colloquies*, or rather conversations (in fact, it consists of relatively short dialogues on various topics) had, as the author intended, two goals; namely, first, the development of the command of Latin, especially in its practical applications, and second, training of different moral virtues, especially wisdom, which is one of the virtues since Aristotle.[12] The key to understanding these conversations, which are seemingly trivial but, in fact, deal with the most important problems of life, is the form in which he related the moral message – it is the so called *paragone*, i.e., a comparison of all kinds of attitudes, behaviours, beliefs, etc. with one another, and leading the reader or listener along a path that would lead him to one of the virtues. Certainly,

---

[8] Cf. J. Burckhardt, *The Civilization of the Renaissance in Italy*, London 1928, p. 254.

[9] "In short, the appreciation of the joys of life, which Erasmus manifests, is fairly cool; moreover, he soon changed his mood of hopeful expectation, never to find it again. However, compared with current feeling in the preceding century, except in Italy, Erasmus's appreciation might rather be called warm." Cf. J. Huizinga, *The Waning of the Middle Ages*, London 1987, p. 31.

[10] Cf. P. Kondylis, *Die Aufklärung im Rahmen des neuzeitlichen Rationalismus*, Stuttgart 1981, p. 124 ff.

[11] They were written most probably in 1497-1500 (although they were first published in 1518) to teach language and ethics to university youth in the department of liberal arts (*artes liberals*). In a classic (or Parisian) university organization there were four departments, that is: arts, law, medicine, and theology. "The faculty of arts, greater in numbers than the other faculties, was based on a system of nations. The professors and students formed groups which roughly corresponded to their place of origin. In Paris, there are four nations: French, Picardian, Norman, and English." Cf. J. Le Goff, *Intellectuals in the Middle Ages*, Oxford 1993, p. 70.

[12] Kristeller reminds us that already by the "thirteenth century all works of Aristotle have been translated into Latin and were widely used in Paris and other universities as philosophy textbooks." In the next century, "the doctrines of Aristotle on virtues and the highest good, as well as his theory of emotions presented in the *Rhetoric*, were well known by students of philosophy and many other readers. Since the fifteenth century, a significant part of ethics and general writings on morality were based on the works of Aristotle, whose significant advantage was the exhaustive approach to the topic and abundance of detail." [...] in the sixteenth century, practical life rules begin to dominate, along with descriptions of customs and habits." Cf. P. O. Kristeller, *Humanizm i filozofia*, op. cit., p. 102 ff.

this form of moralism was taken over from ancient rhetoric. However, the Renaissance humanists "hammered" it into the reality of contemporary life, and some of them, including Erasmus, added to it their intellectual passion in tracking what constituted a negation of some particular virtues or all the virtues taken together.[13]

Already the first of these conversations – between Arnold and Cornelius, who was returning from a pilgrimage to Jerusalem – touches a problem that Erasmus considered to be most important. It is the matter of manifestations of stupidity (ignorance) and wisdom. This matter was put by him in clear opposition to the beliefs and behaviours that were dominant at that time. When Arnold asks his friend, in his "slovenly dress, lean carcase, and ghastly phyz," where he comes from, the other replies that he was in the "other world." However, to the question what he saw there, he replied that he saw "a great deal of Barbarity." In turn, to the question: "What winds blew thee thither," he replies that it was folly – the same one which "blows a great many other Folks thither." From this short conversation we can also learn about other forms of stupidity, for example, such as faith in the power of a "big goblet that after a toast was drunk became a full votive offering of honour – a gift to a saint" or in the power of indulgences (they did not help the pilgrim attacked on the road by robbers, even though he "had a whole satchel full of indulgences").[14] From this conversation flow at least several different wisdoms. The first, and most obvious one, is the wisdom "sadder but wiser;" the second is the "the wisdom of one ashamed" with his gullibility, and finding no excuse for it. The third one is relatively most profound; it is the "wisdom of the detached" from commonplace beliefs and mental simpletons, but also from the seemingly wise and sophisticated church officials (they "sell bulls there to dead men too"). Such signs of stupidity are also present in other colloquies.

In a conversation on the *Pilgrimage for religion's sake*, clearly satirical and sarcastic accents are added; because how else to read the image of Ogygius returning from a pilgrimage, ringed with "scallop shells," "tin and leaden images," "straw necklaces," "snake eggs on [his] arms," and satisfied that he had completed the mission appointed to him by his mother in law, to "pay his respects to St. James and thank him in person" for the delivery of a child by his wife. One of the new elements is a suggestion which appears in it that one can

---

[13] "The favourite play in humanist literature was rhetorical argument about the primacy of one of some opposites or rivals. [...] This was the manner in which the advantage and superiority of some forms of art, professions or modes of life were discussed. There are treatises on "the sword and the quill" which deal with the positive aspects of a military and literary life." Cf. ibidem, p. 131.

[14] Cf. Erasmsus, *Colloquies*, Chicago 1878, p. 51.

remain a fool in one respect or – which is just the same – maintain the mentality of a naive simpleton and in some other respect get rid of this naivety under the influence of life experience. Ogygius is such a case. He maintains deep belief in the power of St. James and other saints and holy items (such as, for example, a letter circulating among the faithful, which the "Virgin Mary herself wrote"), but not in those of many ordinary people who live off of pilgrims and pilgrimages (such as those "greedy tavern keepers who, though they won't serve a decent meal, don't hesitate to charge their guests outrageous prices"[15]).

In these dialogues the motif of the stupidity of scholars is also exposed. In a conversation between the abbot and "a learned lady," the former argues that "it's not feminine to be brainy. A lady's business is to have a good time," and to lead a pleasant life, which, in fact, means idleness, and – and what is not less important – it is not befitting a lady to look for wisdom in books. This "learned lady", however, does just that and it does not look as if the abbot has convinced her to abandon this activity. He does convince her, however, that "once, an unenlightened abbot was an exception yet today he is common." In a conversation about *Exorcisms, or the Specter* an apparent wisdom is shown in those conducting exorcisms (they are not fools but clever charlatans making up fairy tales about possessions and knowing their job perfectly, i.e., magic tricks), and those who are the object of their practices and those who believe in their fairy tales (they are the real fools). In a conversation about *Alchemy,* these tricksters are, of course, alchemists, while the real fools are those who – like the old man "mad about the art called alchemy" (although he "let himself be duped in an extraordinary manner") – have invariably believed in the art of transforming "coal into gold." In the conversation about *The Tricked Trickster*, although Erasmus suggests that every cheater can be caught at some point, his argumentation presented here is not so very convincing.

Manifestations of ignorance, condemned in the *Colloquies*, are also the subject of criticism in the *Praise of Folly*. Obviously, the title of this treaty is sarcastic. In an address to Thomas More preceding it, the author declares that he wants to "entertain the reader rather than bite him," but the stupidity presented in it – both on the whole and in individual incarnations – makes one rather sad than happy; after all is there anything funny in the statement that "about Folly (written by Erasmus with a capital letter), even greatest fools talk" or that "folly itself should be the trumpet of her glory" and "it is the same what is done by some seemingly great and wise men", who "propose [themselves] as a complete pattern of all virtues, from each of which he is yet as far distant as heaven itself from hell." This is just the overture to the great concert called the

---

[15] Cf. Erasmus, *Colloquies*, vol. 1, Toronto 1997, p. 619.

Praise of Folly.[16] It is followed by a short list of those who have historic merit in propagating stupidity. The first ones listed are the Stoics ("the next place to gods is challenged by the Stoics"), while the second place is taken by the Pythagoreans (they made up this mysterious "quarters," which was supposed to explain the source of all life). After these and similar "crabbed philosophers," there are "monks and friars" (including "Popes"), "old men" ("they are freed from such vexations as would torment them if they were more wise") and, similar to them, children talking gibberish ("their prattling, their playing, their short memory, their heedlessness, and all their other endowments"). The list also includes "the youth," the people of Brabant, who stand out from other nations with their stupidity ("the more ancient they grow, the more foolish they are"), silly ("by definition") women ("that which made Plato doubt under what genus to rank women, whether among brutes or rational creatures, was only meant to denote the extreme stupidness and Folly of that sex"), ancient and modern grammarians, dialecticians and rhetoricians (their art is reduced to "litigation in courts"), and physicians ("in this profession, those that have most confidence, though the least skill, shall be sure of the greatest custom"), and lawyers; "thus divines may bite their nails, and naturalists may blow their fingers, astrologers may know their own fortune is to be poor" ("While all these hard-named fellows cannot make so great a figure as a single quack").

Roughly in the middle of the treatise, there is a statement which suggests that Erasmus had had enough of this indicating of groups of fools and he aims at general conclusions. He states here, among other things, that fools live a happy life: "an additional happiness of these fools appears farther in this, that when they have run merrily on to their last stage of life, they neither find any fear nor feel any pain to die, but march contentedly to the other world, where their company must surely be as acceptable as it was upon earth. Let us draw now a comparison between the condition of a fool and that of a wise man, and see how infinitely the one outweighs the other. Give me any instance then, of a man as wise as you can fancy him possible to be, that has spent all his younger years poring over books, and trudging after learning, in the pursuit whereof he squanders away the pleasantest time of his life in watching, sweating and fasting; and in his latter days he never tastes one mouthful of delight..."[17] It turns out further on that this wise man is not a fully positive character: he looks rather poorly ("always stingy poor, dejected," "pale, lean, thin-jawed, sickly"), and what he does and says signals some form of madness ("alas, this is but a fallacy"). Although Erasmus ensures that this madness must be distinguished

---

[16] Cf. Erasmus, *The Praise of Folly*, New York 1922, p. 29.
[17] Cf. ibidem, p. 133.

from the madness of all the aforementioned fools ("there is a certain difference in the nature [of the madness]") and to confirm this he refers to the then
most important authorities – such as Plato, who placed frenzy "among the
particular goods of life," or Cicero, who longed for such a folly ("madness")
and asked: "does welcome frenzy make thus mistake?", madness is madness
and – in the opinion of Erasmus – "the greater each man's madness is, the
greater is his happiness, if it be but such a sort as proceeds from an excess in
folly, which is so epidemical a distemper that it is hard to find any one man
so uninfected as not to have sometimes a fit or two of some sort of frenzy."

In the next part of his dissertation, Erasmus tries to convince the reader
that, although it is impossible to be completely free from folly ("madness"),
one can and should at least defend oneself against those forms which most
obviously escape common sense, e.g., "if anyone be so short-sighted as to
take a mule for an ass, or so shallow-pated as to admire a paltry ballad for an
elegant poem" or when "he whose wife is a common jilt, that keeps a ware-
house free for all customers, and yet swears she is as chaste as an untouched
virgin, and hugs himself in his contented mistake," or ... (Of course, there are
a lot of these "ors"). However, Erasmus very much wanted not only to make
up a list of the worst cases of stupidity, but he also wanted to distinguish the
ones which were more harmful from those which were less harmful. What
is more, he made an attempt at categorizing them, i.e., identifying groups of
half wisdoms, quarter wisdoms and stupidity. One of them is the "wisdoms"
of particular nations – like "The English challenge the prerogative of having
the most handsome women, of being the most accomplished in the science
of music, and of keeping the best tables. The Scotch brag of their gentility,
pretend the genius of their native soil inclines them to be good disputants.
The French think themselves remarkable for complaisance and good breed-
ing." There are certainly some great collective "follies," but these are not some
eternal truths, universal, or even only shared by the majority of wise people.

In fact, there are supposedly not too many of them in the world – if any
will be found at all: "The Grecians, it is true, reckoned up seven within the
narrow precincts of their own country." After words promising another enu-
meration of the signs of stupidity, questions appear about that which can and
that which cannot be regarded as a sign of wisdom, as well as how hard it is
for a wise person to be wise (because even the wisest of men can, for example,
"be mad about some woman and the less she loves him back the madder he
is") and how difficult it is to find among different people a wise one, and
how easy it is for a fool to be stupid and how well fare the representatives of
"stupid guilds." "The most stupid and dirtiest of all is the merchants' guild"
(and how much "gold they have on their stubby fingers"), and yet there are

also grammarians ("a sort of men who would be the most miserable, the most slavish, and the most hateful of all persons"), poets ("the whole intent of their profession is only to smooth up and tickle the ears of fools, [and] that by mere toys and fabulous shams"), rhetoricians ("they will sometimes as it were mutter their words inwardly"), masters of epistolary art ("these coxcombs employ their pens in writing congratulatory epistles, poems and panegyrics, upon each other"), "those who pass on the work of others as their own and they pass on the glory gained by someone else's great effort to themselves just like jugglers," lawyers ("they will cite you six hundred precedents, though not one of them come near to the case in hand"), "then come philosophers, venerable thanks to their beards and long coats" (but not thanks to their minds), theologians ("perhaps it would be better if I passed them over in silence," but it must be said of them at least so much that it is harder to get from this whole heap of different scholastic systems than from a maze") etc. In the conclusion to this list of "wise" people in their own ways, but considered by Erasmus as fools, he wrote: "fortune we find still favouring the blunt, and flushing the forward; strokes and smoothes up fools, crowning all their undertakings with success; but wisdom makes her followers bashful, sneaking, and timorous, and therefore you see that they are commonly reduced to hard shifts, must grapple with poverty, cold and hunger, must lie recluse, despised, and unregarded, while fools roll in money, are advanced to dignities and offices, and in a word have the whole world at command."[18]

Erasmus' dissertations quoted so far can be treated as essays written by an experienced writer – in some places they are witty, malicious, sarcastic and intellectually perverse (if you can call something which at the beginning of an argument seems to be praise, and at the end it turns out to be a rebuke), but still these are essays based so much on observation of everyday life and the thoughts of the author, and their author often gladly reaches for the so-called strong words and terse similes. It is different in the case of his *Ratio vera theologiae* (*Method of True Theology*), a treatise written in connection with the translation of *The New Testament* made by Erasmus (from Greek into Latin) and published in 1517. Perhaps this work may not be a classical scholastic treatise, however, it has at least some of its characteristics, such as references to sources (primarily, *The Vulgate*), or terminological explanations and clarifications. It was the intention of Erasmus that *The Method of True Theology* was to be "a sufficiently extensive preface" to *The New Testament* which he published. However, he would not be himself if he did not add (just at the very beginning): "I shall give my work such proportions that it can be a preface, if someone prefers this, but

---

[18] Cf. ibidem, p. 273.

if not, so that it can be read separately. In doing so I imitate those hosts who like splendour and are thrifty at the same time, and who mix the leftovers of yesterday with fresh food and spice them with a popular seasoning." Of course, there is some sarcasm, but also intellectual perversity in this. The latter becomes increasingly evident in the course of reading this dissertation.[19]

The dissertation is directly addressed to those who were "candidates to sacred theology," who were taught at the Trilingual College of the University of Louvain (within it there were chairs in Greek, Latin and Hebrew, and Erasmus was one of its professors); these candidates were to be brought by a shorter, simpler and more reliable road to the goal to which aimed and still aim all students of theology. Indirectly, however, it is addressed to all the followers of this theology – both those more and less learned as well as people "simple and of humble origins, of not very deep minds." Answering the question: "What do they all need?," Erasmus replied that they needed many different things; among others, "sincere and profound faith, which sees only this which is divine. They also need a great eagerness to learn. As this incomparable treasury will not endure either ordinary or commonplace love, or that would be loved on par with the other things. It calls for the hungry spirit and the one which desires nothing but itself." Neither this nor anything else these candidates and followers of sacred theology will achieve if they cannot accede to it with "the mind worthy of it, not only as far as possible, pure from every stain of sin, but also peaceful and safe from all the hustle and bustle of desires, because thanks to it the more clearly will be reflected in us, as if in a smooth and polished mirror, the image of this eternal Truth." The method proposed by Erasmus, in its author's intention, is not to free oneself from "every trace of sin," but only from certain types of sins, including the sin of foolishness.

The issue of how foolishness is manifested in theologians is present in many pages of the dissertation. At its very beginning he writes about such habits of some theologians which "make it that this most pious vocation sometimes has a bad name. This is because if these theologians reached such high honours in their state, they sometimes become more insolent than the average brothers, and also more greedy for honours, quicker to get angry, more vicious in the language they use, in general in all ordinary circumstances of life not only more burdensome than simpletons, but also more troublesome than they would normally be themselves, so these and those think that this was theology that made them such."[20]

---

[19] Cf. Erazm z Rotterdamu, *Sposób, czyli metoda szybkiego i łatwego dochodzenia do prawdziwej teologii*, in: idem, *Trzy rozprawy*, Warsaw 1960, p. 63 ff.

[20] Ibidem, p. 70.

However, the main purpose of this dissertation is not to list the behaviours that were an embarrassment to theologians and theology but to show the way leading to "[wisdom in] theological truth." The word "method," used in the title, turns out to be such a process of the education of minds, in which there are to be discovered or established such truths that protect against prejudice, superstition or falsehood. After all, this is the same method which Erasmus used in other works, e.g., in the *Praise of Folly*, by leading the readers to the pursued objective by giving positive and negative examples. Its theological specificity in the *Theological Method* consists in that wisdom is not represented by fictional characters, but mostly by the well-known and recognized religious authorities. From time to time in this dissertation there are references to some famous philosopher or such "an illustrious man" of whom only a few have heard, which is a pity, because he had contributed, even if not in attaining theological wisdom, at least in supporting those who either seek to attain it, or those who disseminate it.[21]

Therefore, in this work we have such notables as: "Saint James, who admonishes that the one who has achieved true wisdom, shared and proclaimed it not in pride, not in tough dispute, but in righteousness, morals and kindness;" St. Augustine, who "when conducting a dispute with Cresconius [...] when his opponent quoted a testimony from Ecclesiastes, whose meaning was ridiculous, recommended him to turn to the Greek as it was there that he might seek a more sure;" and Origen – who although not a saint, still he talked in such a "refined" manner and with such a sense that Erasmus could "show on a myriad of examples how boring – not to say ridiculous – some rave, whenever a saint is to be celebrated with a song of praise or to use a form of the hymn, which requires brilliance and feelings. We owe just to this kind of theologians some such hymns and church songs, which people call sequences, and which no man educated in literature can read without laughter or disgust."[22]

At this point we come to the Erasmian blacklist – stupidity, ugliness, bad taste etc. It is made up not so much of a gallery of characters (although some names also appear in it from time to time), but rather as a kind of collection of cultural symbols (such as the biblical "Pharisees, scribes and the rich") and of key-words indicating the places where these negative figures can be easily found – with words such as "a certain theologian" or "our newer theologian."[23]

---

[21] Such as the honourable Hieronymus Buslidius who "in his will donated a large sum of money to this end, so that people who were to teach three languages at Louvain could receive a decent salary."

[22] Cf. ibidem, p. 86 ff.

[23] Erasmus, when trying to rationalize this escape into generality, says that "at the moment he does not mean to disclose somebody's ignorance, but to encourage youth to use the best

3. Michel Montaigne

Essays (fr. for trail, attempt), by Michel Montaigne (1533-1592), is a work consisting of three large volumes and is considered to be one of the most significant achievements of the French Renaissance. But the problem is that it is impossible to answer unequivocally the question of what is so important, or interesting in them. It is not only that the author had many different things to say, but it depends here on who is looking, how he is looking and what he is looking for. Those who have approached this work from the standpoint of the traditions of scepticism or libertarianism have found here mainly those motifs which continue those traditions and pave the way forward.[24] Those who have sought in them genuine religion and religiosity found tips which, in their opinion, could and should lead to such religion and religiosity.[25] However, before both these groups found what they were seeking in the *Essays*, they had to deal with the specific form of conveying the messages, which is seemingly a chatty one, but is in fact intellectually perverse, because it combines light joking with rather a bitter saying of "yes" in order to say "no" (or the other way around), and putting trivial things next to fundamental ones.[26]

For those who are looking for answers to the question of Montaigne's standards of rationality, his liberal operating with reasons is particularly difficult, so much so that at some moment one may doubt whether these reasons

---

methods. I shall tell generally only as much on the matter that if someone wants to have its proof at once, let him compare those old theologians such as Origenes, Basilius, Chrisostome, Hieronymus with our recent ones." Ibidem, p. 87.

[24] Cf. J.S. Spink, *French Free-Thought from Gassendi to Voltaire*, London 1960, p. 3 ff. Rolf Elberfeld sees in Montaigne not only a continuer of Skeptic traditions ("his philosophy does not allow any explicit opinion and forces to doubt constantly") but also pessimistic traditions; in any case, those which reduce philosophy to "the art of dying." Cf. R. Elberfeld, *Was ist Philosophie? Programmatische Texte von Platon bis Derrida*, Stuttgart 2006, p. 119 ff.

[25] One such readers of the *Essays* was Blaise Pascal – in his *Thoughts* he refers to Montaigne (whom he treats as an authority) on several occasions; "What good there is in Montaigne can only have been acquired with difficulty. The evil that is in him, I mean apart from his morality, could have been corrected in a moment, if he had been informed that he made too much of trifles and spoke too much of himself." Cf. B. Pascal, *Thoughts*, New York 1910, p. 24.

[26] Raymond Lebègue, when characterizing the book, writes that it "discourages its readers with its content and form," and its contradictions ("easily spotted"), and its "overlapping of layers" (this is due to "reediting the text in 1580, 1588, and 1958-92"). Cf. A. Adam, Montaigne in: *Literatura francuska*, t. I, Warsaw 1974, p. 252. It must be added that writing the *Essays* took Montaigne a total of 20 years – first (approx. 10 years) he prepared to write the text (by studying works of antiquity and the Renaissance and making notes on his observations around him), and later (after the first edition of 1580), he reedited the work and expounded on several fragments (yet leaving the form of the first edition intact).

are treated seriously and whether they are worthy of a philosopher's attention. However, it should be said at the start that Montaigne's words should not always be taken literally – for example, if only to refer to one declaration in his address to the Reader: "Thus, reader, myself and the matter of my book: there's no reason thou shouldst employ thy leisure on so frivolous and vain subject."[27]

Apparently the answer to the question what he generally means is simple and obvious. From the words preceding this declaration it is clear in fact that he means acquiring wisdom by himself and the possible passing of it on to others, but without the wish to instruct or to teach anything to anybody, or even "seek the world›s favour" (for some recognition or for honours). It is only a careful reading of the subsequent books and chapters of the *Essays* that convinces us that this is not the only and most important of meanings. One of its central issues is human wisdom (rationality), but it turns out that different roads lead to it and it has different forms ("facets"), and, despite being (or perhaps just because of that fact) so desired by many, it behaves like a capricious lady – once getting up on the right foot, and sometimes on the left; sometimes being in high spirits and sometimes in low ones. Of course, this is only a metaphor, but a metaphor that seems to reflect well the general intent, message and ideas of this voluminous work.

Montaigne writes about the different forms ("facets") of wisdom in practically every chapter of the *Essays*, and it should be said that in one respect they complement one another, in another they are mutually exclusive, and quite often they complement and exclude each other at the same time. After all, this suggestion appears already in the title of Chapter I of the first volume – it is stated there that "by different methods men arrive at the same end", and this goal can be either practising some virtue (let's say such as wisdom), or to obtain by its means of some other goal in life (such as inner peace or cheerfulness), or... etc. In short, "man (in good earnest) is a marvellous, vain, fickle, and unstable subject, on whom it is very hard to form any certain and uniform judgement." This is obviously some philosophical wisdom, or at least one of those wisdoms that have any characteristics of philosophical wisdom.

Of course, other types appear in later chapters. And so, in the second chapter Montaigne tells about great sadness and great joy, and that both these feelings in an exaggerated form turn out to be equally harmful (as in the case of Pope Leo X, who, after receiving news of the capture of Milan, "was rapt with so sudden an excess of joy that he immediately fell into a fever and died," hence the conclusion that "all passions that suffer themselves to be relished and digested are but moderate"). In chapter three he says, among other things,

---

[27] Cf. M. Montaigne, *Essays*, vol. 1, London 1902, p. 3.

that at one time "wisdom is satisfied with what is," at another time it is satisfied with that "what one desires." One time wisdom "is glad" of one thing and another time of the other thing; hence it was from this that the Platonic great warning: "Do thine own work, and know thyself" came. In chapter four, it is said, among other things, that "the soul, being transported and discomposed, turns its violence upon itself, if not supplied with something to oppose." Chapter five states, among other things, that although "it is reputed a victory of less glory to overcome by force than by fraud," in practice it is the latter that achieves triumphs rather than the first one. However, let us not get caught up in this kind of reasoning proposed by Montaigne – although in this way we would learn about different wisdoms, sometimes amusing, sometimes amazing and sometimes inclining to deeper reflection, but rather we will not learn everything about human greatness (if such exists) and smallness (there are too many kinds of it to doubt its existence), nor shall we manage to capture a relatively logically coherent sense of these arguments.

However, we can try to sort out these arguments according to the general topics appearing in them. In this work at least seven such motifs appear. The first one – relatively the most prominent – is the motif of the diversity and variety of human opinions; the second is that of the relativity of human rationality and unreasonableness; the third is that of human passion; the fourth is that of conflicts inherent in human nature; the fifth one is that of free will; the sixth of different people's being the subject to different conditions; while the seventh is balancing all the previous ones – the motif of the discrepancy between the world of human nature and the world of human culture. Of course, such terms as "ordering" or "balancing" in the case of this work have been and probably will remain debatable. We must therefore let it be (because otherwise we would have to return to the Montaignean "or").

By developing the topic of the variety and diversity of human opinions Montaigne tries to show that there are so many of them that "tis impossible to find two opinions exactly alike, not only in several men, but in the same man, at diverse hours." First, this is because "objects have different facets and different perspectives", which means that they are subject to different changes and in these changes they reveal their different properties, and second, the senses have limited perceptual abilities, which means that they "capture" at random this or that, and third, the human imagination turns out to be misleading (as an example can be a philosopher in a small cage "on the top of the high tower of Notre Dame of Paris," who is confused and frightened although he is completely safe). The conclusion which generalizes these considerations amounts to saying that every opinion is relative, i.e., is not just simply true or false, but at one time it may be regarded as true and at other times as false, and there is no contradiction in this, because everything depends on one's point of view, or on the so-called circumstances.

Developing the topic of the relativity of human rationality and unreasonableness, Montaigne seeks to demonstrate that human knowledge should not be seen solely or even primarily in terms of logic (truth and falsehood, clarity and confusion, etc.), because "truth and falsehood have the same face," i.e., what to one person is clear to another is unclear, and there is no reliable way to identify a logical criteria that would be reliable and possible to accept. However, one can and even should consider rationality and stupidity also in pragmatic terms such as, for example, usefulness and uselessness. Of course, they are also of a relative character. For example, for "ordinary people," what turns out to be most useful is "common knowledge" which consists of beliefs that are not only mutually exclusive but also contrary to the "knowledge of scientists." The latter seems to be internally consistent to those scientists, of course, until they find the contradictions inherent in it, and it is very likely that eventually one of them will find them.

While developing the topic of human passions, Montaigne seeks, among other things, to show that one of those passions is the pursuit of truth. While recognizing that "there is no more natural desire than lust for knowledge," he admits to this not to praise or justify it, but in order to show how contradictory are human desires and aspirations. For there is also no "more natural desire" than that of inner peace, and "the desire to know" raises concerns rather than peace.

Directly connected with the theme of human passions is the topic of the conflicting character of human nature. Expanding on this, Montaigne tries to show that the fundamental sources of all human conflicts are inherent in human nature – in his "arrogance" ("a congenital and primary disease"), in his pride (e.g., it leads him to be rather a "leader of a stray mob than a pupil in the school of truth"), vanity (prompts him, among other things, to trust one's individual forces rather than the collective ones of mankind), etc. To those who are trying to remedy something with the help of reason, he advises "to first try to reconcile reason with itself" (and this appears to be unfeasible). But to those who attempt to remedy this by establishing new rules of social life, he says that "there is nothing so dangerous for the state than innovation" ("change only lends shape to injustice and tyranny").

Developing the topic of free will, Montaigne seeks to show that as a rule people make bad use of freedom. It serves, amongst others, the "debauchery of thought," "granting oneself the right of various judgement, selection of and adherence to a party," committing various offences (against laws, customs, etc.), and, to make matters worse, of excusing them. In short, free will turns out to be lawlessness. This conclusion leads the author of the *Essays* to formulate a thesis that happy are not those who are free, but those who are enslaved ("happy is the nation that does what it is bid to do without having to worry about its reason"). He also wrote a chapter about saving the will in which he states, among other things, that "the career of our desires ought to be circumscribed and restrained to a short limit of the nearest and most continuous commodities." A little further and he added, "we must play our part properly."[28]

On the topic of various conditionings, Montaigne especially focused on the issue of man being "possessed" by "trivial reasons" ("the most trivial things make people veer around in their judgements, decisions and actions"), i.e., by "lust, anger, amusement and jealousy", and by external "things," such as "air quality" (weather).

All this is to lead to radical divergences between human nature and culture. A confirmation of such differences is human speech – it should serve to express what is, yet is used to "puff little things," "distorting and debauching the very essence of things," "awarding without merit and as one likes of the most praiseworthy adjectives" etc. This is also confirmed by customs – they should be natural, but they are bizarre, amazing and sometimes amusing – like in the case of customs of greeting and farewell (this "kissing of hands, and snake-like bowing and skips" etc.).

In each book of the *Essays* there can be found descriptions of such customs, which to an observer from the outside may seem to be contrary to reason, but which are treated by persons practising them as totally rational and socially justified. For example, in Chapter XVII of the first book, he points out, among other things, "the custom of the kings of Persia to give their lieutenants and agents so little rein, that, upon the least arising difficulties, they must fain have recourse to their further commands; this delay, in so vast an extent of dominion, having often very much prejudiced their affairs." In turn, in the third chapter in the second book he also writes about the habits of the Greeks and Romans, such as suicide (in its light "the most voluntary death is the finest").[29]

---

[28] "[...] but withal as a part of a borrowed personage; we must not make real essence of a mask and outward appearance." Cf. Montaigne, *The Complete Essays of Michel de Montaigne*, vol. 2, London 1910, p. 532. This "but" contains as much of Montaigne as his provocative thesis saying that an enslaved man lives a better life than a free man.

[29] "But (!!!) this does not pass without admitting a dispute: for many are of opinion that we cannot quit this garrison of the world without the express command of Him who has placed us in it; and that it appertains to God who has placed us here, not for ourselves only but for His Glory and the service of others, to dismiss us when it shall best please Him." Cf. ibidem, p. 21. These "many" are of course Christians, to whom suicide is a breach of divine command.

Of course, wise men (thoughtful and acting rationally) perceive these and many other divergences and adopt such manners that are consistent with reason; but with their own reason. Some part of the answer to the question what kind of reason it is, can be found in chapter XXXVI of Book Two, which is entitled: *The Most Excellent Men*. Montaigne presented there a short list of these "most excellent men" – the first of them is Homer (his books have become "most perfect things, most perfect instructor in the knowledge of all things," "a treasury of all sorts of learning"), in the second place there is Alexander the Great ("for his manners, in general, seem in truth incapable of any manner of reproach") together with Julius Caesar, and "in the third and most splendid place" – Epaminondas (although "of glory he has not near so much as the other two [...]; of valour and resolution, not of that sort which is pushed on by ambition, but that which wisdom and reason can plant in a regular soul, he had all that could be imagined. [...] But as to his manners and conscience, he infinitely surpassed all men" and "comes not short of any philosopher whatever, not even of Socrates himself").[30]

On the basis of this brief and – needless to say – controversial list of "the most excellent people" we can come to a conclusion that what counts in man are reason and rationality, but not only these but also "fortitude and courage", and many other attributes of the mind and body, and that which of them becomes important or more important than others depends on whether individual or collective life is involved, and also so many more external circumstances that even the greatest philosophers could not enumerate.

Of the different "fors" and "againsts" presented in the *Essays*, a Montaignean "prudent man" (*honnete homme*) emerges, i.e., someone who is neither presumptuous, neither good hearted, neither impertinent nor flattering, neither an avenger nor ... (certainly, we could go on quoting his personal traits). What is most important in him is that, depending on the situation, he is more of the first or of the second or of the third or of the fourth quality, etc., and also that he treats all of these incarnations as a mask that he puts on when playing any of the roles in this great spectacle of human life. However, he distances himself (just like a professional actor) from any of these roles, and – if possible – from the entire performance in which he is forced to take part. For such a person virtually everything is neither true nor false, neither good nor bad, neither just nor unjust, neither... (it is already well known what is meant later on).

---

[30] "Innocence, in this man, is a quality peculiar, sovereign, constant, uniform, incorruptible, compared with which, it appears in Alexander subject to something else subaltern, uncertain, variable, effeminate, and fortuitous." Ibidem, p. 268. Epaminondas (c. 410 – 362 BCE) was a Theban statesman and leader who crushed the military dominance of Sparta (in 371 BCE he defeated the Spartan army in the battle of Leuctra).

One of the life mottoes of this man was contained in Montaigne's statement: "a wise man ought, within, to withdraw and retire his soul from the crowd and there keep it at liberty and in power to judge freely of things; but as to externals, absolutely to follow and conform himself to the fashion of the time." In practice, this is manifested in demonstrating submission to the already existing beliefs, customs, laws, authorities, etc. on the outside, but on the inside in opposing to "the curbs imposed by them" ("unless coercion and slavery are useful"). This man will say what is commonly said, and will say it in the way it is publicly said, that is, ambiguously and evasively (often making use of: "perhaps," "to some extent," "they say," "I suppose," etc.), unless the circumstances allow him to express his beliefs explicitly (although this happens rarely). This man will rather defend the already existing forms of life and human coexistence and will stand against all kinds of newsmongers, but he will not be doing it because they seem to him to be reasonable, good or fair, but because he is convinced that maintaining these forms of behaviour would be beneficial to him as well as to those with whom he had to coexist ("in public affairs there is no such bad order if it were long eternal and permanent, which would be worth more than changes and shocks"). Of course, he would say different things in public and privately, and he would even say that "one should not make a show of one's own private opinions." However, if someone accuses him that in this way he turns out to be a hypocrite, an opportunist, or a conformist, he would either admit it (if he finds that it does not involve any danger to him), or he would be looking for some rational justification of such behaviour, or trying to convince this person that his behaviour has nothing to do with such faults.

Postscript

In each of the thinkers cited here we find some implications of standards of rationality in the philosophical and religious traditions of the time, as well as in the ongoing processes of profound change in intellectual culture. In the case of Nicholas of Cusa these are mainly implications in the changes taking place in the Renaissance Christian theology. According to Etienne Gilson, they were also implicated in the medieval mystical tradition, especially in the mysticism of Meister Eckhart – according to this historian, the author of *On Learned Ignorance* applied in his standards of rationality "theological principles of Eckhard" including the principle of *reductio ad nihilo* (reduction to nothingness) and the principle of *reductio ad absurdum* (reduction to absurdity). He is supposed to have done this by his desire of defending Christianity, which – in the opinion of this historian – had been in peril.[31] The source of this threat was supposedly in the disputes among academic philosophers and theologians. Therefore, he wanted to convince them to "consider their disputes as [an] unimportant difference of opinion in philosophy and theology," and shift from their dogmatic stance to a critical one ("Nicolas was clever enough to perceive that the trouble with those men was that they were all equally dogmatic, no less in their negations than in their assertions"). I agree with E. Gilson on two issues, namely, first, that the intellectual core of Cusanian rationality is a peculiar dialectic of negation and affirmation (of putting more emphasis on negation rather than affirmation), and second, that in the sphere of motivation there is a clash between religious motifs and philosophical ones and that ultimately the former dominate. Of course, it is difficult to clearly identify what is their advantage over philosophical motifs. According to E. Gilson, the advantage is so great that it leads to "a complete renunciation of philosophy as a discipline based on reason."[32] This thesis raises my serious objections.

Also in Erasmus of Rotterdam we are dealing with a specific dialectics of negation and affirmation and with a peculiar struggle for the primacy of philosophical motives with religious ones. In his various treatises, his dialectics as well as the clash of philosophical and religious motives assume different forms. However, in none of them does Erasmus leave any doubt that his standards of rationality contain more philosophical than theological wisdom and in this there is more affinity to the ancient philosophical authorities than the ecclesiastical ones. In Erasmus's discourses, Plato and Aristotle are mentioned relatively frequently. But in any case, recognition of their philosophy, philosophizing and their behaviour in their lives is combined with some criticism (negation). For example, in *Praise of Folly* he refers to Plato as the philosopher who accurately "described this philosophy as an examination of death." However, he presents him there also as a man of such timidity that in a situation where he should defend Socrates, "he was so scared by the clamour of the crowd that he barely managed to cough out the beginning of the first sentence" (in *Apology of Socrates* – A/N).[33] In the *Method of Theology* Plato and Aristotle compete for the position of the greatest authority. At the end, the former seems to be gaining the upper hand, but this advantage is obtained, among other things, thanks to the fact that, at least up to some point in time, he followed the path laid out by his predecessors. Moreover, before and after Aristotle, such philosophers appeared who first followed one of their Masters, and later made a step or several steps forward in philosophical wisdom (ra-

---

[31] Cf. E. Gilson, *The Unity of Philosophical Experience*, New York 1950, p. 13.
[32] Cf. ibidem, p. 112 ff.
[33] Cf. Erasmus, *The Praise of Folly*, op. cit., p. 202.

tionality). Thus, this method – first of following the already laid out path and later abandoning it and following one's own path – fits within the standards of Erasmian rationality.[34]

The clash between religious and philosophical motifs in Montaigne's *Essays* is the relatively weakest. This does not mean that their author was a religiously neutral man. There are many indications that he was in his own way attached to the religion by which he was raised. However, a lot also indicates that he did not feel competent to speak in public on matters of religion. However, he felt competent to speak out on philosophical matters, and that to him meant above all the expression of critical opinions (according to him "to philosophize meant the same as to doubt") about philosophers and philosophy. This is confirmed on many pages of his *Essays*, and the extensive discussion and justification of this approach he presented in Chapter II of the Second Book, entitled *Apology for Raymond Sebond*. Montaigne reduced all of the so-called (by him) "philosophical sects" to "three major schools," "two make explicit confession of doubt and ignorance; in the dogmatic school, i.e., the third one, it is easy to discover that the majority put only the mask of confidence, to put on a brave face", but (!!!) somehow it was not easy for Montaigne to believe that "Epicurus, Plato and Pythagoras gave us for current coin their Atoms, their Ideas and their Numbers; they were too wise to establish their articles of faith upon matter so uncertain and so debatable." But it is easier for him to believe that they wrote some things to satisfy their natural curiosity, while others "for the needs of the community" and "showed in it considerable prudence in that that they did go too much against common opinions..." In turn, about "the philosophers of doubt and ignorance" (such as the Pyrrhonists or Academics from the second and third Platonic Academy) he wrote that "they cannot express their general concept in any manner of speaking," "so that when they say 'I doubt', one can immediately squeeze their throats and force them to confess that, that they claim and know that they doubt."[35] In short, their doubting and talking about the fact that they doubt, and about what they doubt, is internally contradictory and leads to a contradiction in thinking, speaking and in practical acting, and hence, must be regarded as destructive and autodestructive, i.e., first as lifting diverse affirmations, and then negating itself.

---

[34] "And so Virgil imitated Homer, Theocritus imitated Hesiod, Horace imitated Pindar and Anacreon, Avicenna imitated Galenus, Galenus imitated Hippocrates, Cicero imitated Demosthenes, Xenophon imitated Plato; Aristotle who dealt with everything, in accordance with the subject imitated different authors..." Cf. Erazm z Rotterdamu, *Sposób, czyli metoda...*, op. cit., p. 63 ff.

[35] Ibidem, p. 102.

Of course, Montaigne was against such doubting. Instead, he opted for a prudent doubting that, while freeing us from various types of delusions, illusions and unfounded notions, would still allow in the end to state something quite concrete – maybe not entirely without contradictions, but at least without falling into such contradictions, the removal of which would be possible only when thinking and speaking was renounced. Such doubting grants the right to be placed among the sages to the many ancient philosophers, including the aforementioned Epicure, Plato and Pythagoras, but on condition that they will not be treated as great metaphysicians, logicians, mathematicians, or simply dogmatists, but as writers, poets or, simply, tellers of more or less plausible stories about the world, people, their thoughts and... fabrications.

Today it seems we understand the Montaignean message a little better. Among other things, this is due to postmodernists and the discussions centered on postmodernism. Probably, to some of the representatives or supporters of this philosophical orientation it will be hard to believe, but there are indications that its leading ideas appeared not after modernism, but before modernism. Modernism was often associated by postmodernists with the Enlightenment, and Montaignean rationality was "post" particularly in relation to the medieval intellectual culture. The showcase of that culture is a scholasticism which is based on the formal-logical rules and which, thanks to its accuracy and clarity, promised a solution to all of the most important human issues. A lot can be said about Montaigne's rationality, but not that it continued the scholastic rigour, formalism, or universalism. Just the opposite, his logic is the logic of ambiguity and of demonstrating the uselessness of that which in the eyes of the Scholastics passed as a manifestation of science. Is it not close to postmodernism, which "outdates the scientific belief that science can serve as an arbitrator in all human affairs, setting the only valid cognitive standards, providing a worldview that meets all human needs, determining by their methods the models of rationality."[36] Of course, postmodernists today challenge the validity of that faith in science, which they believe was born during the Enlightenment, and was strengthened in the nineteenth century. However, if you assume that it was based on a conviction about the existence of a foundation of cognition, and also that "it was connected with an expectation that scientific knowledge would bring us closer to understanding some absolute Truth about the world and our place in it," the differences in the outlook as well as epistemological and axiological foundation in understanding of this foundation and the absolute become rather a secondary issue.

---

[36] Cf. A. Szahaj, *Postmodernizm a scjentyzm*, in: *Kultura jako przedmiot badań. Studia filozoficzno-kulturoznawcze*, Poznan 2001, p. 76.

Chapter III

Modern traditions

1. René Descartes

From the very beginning, the philosophy of Descartes (René Descartes, 1596-1650) provoked controversy, but at the same time, influenced generations of modern philosophers.[1] Some of them considered themselves to be its propagators, while others its critical continuators, and still others as critics who completely negated Cartesian rationality.[2] Unfortunately, it is impossible to provide an unambiguous answer to the question about what was, and still is, significant in his philosophy. However, we can point to one element that is indisputable. This is the Cartesian formula: *cogito ergo sum* (I think, therefore I am). Its existence in Cartesianism is undisputed, but its interpretation is disputable – it is disputable even though the formula itself is simple and "self-evident" (as Descartes used to say). But the problem is that, on the basis of Cartesian rationalism, there are no statements which function on their own. They function as components of a philosophical system built by this philosopher from "the very foundations" and which was supposed to enable rational opinions about all that exists or at least could exist in reality, and which would also allow speaking about that which does not exist and cannot exist – not only by saying that it does not exist or that it cannot exist, but also by providing the reasons why something does not exist and cannot exist. At this point already the problem looks fairly complicated, and the deeper we go into Cartesianism, the more complicated the meaning of this formula becomes.

---

[1] [...] his descendants form a numerous and yet diverse group, stretching from the criticism of Kant to Husserl's *Cartesian Meditations*." Cf. G. Rodis-Lewis, *Kartezjusz i racjonalizm*, Warsaw 2000, p. 9 ff.

[2] Ibidem, p. 70.

When trying to answer the question about the standards of Cartesian rationalism, I suggest not to start from this seemingly simple, but in fact very complicated formula implicated in a variety of philosophical contexts. Rather, we will begin with how Descartes viewed himself in the context of philosophical tradition.[3] Such an attempt at self-definition was presented in his *Discourse on the Method*, particularly in its first part. There he expressed his negative assessment of both the humanities on which he had been "brought up since infancy" as well as of his teachers at the Jesuit La Fleche College who educated him. He also admits after graduation: "I found myself involved in so many doubts and errors, that I was convinced I had advanced no farther in all my attempts at learning, than the discovery at every turn of my own ignorance."[4] A little further, his negative evaluation is supplemented by remarks on philosophy ("there is not a single matter within its sphere which is not still in dispute, and nothing, therefore, which is above doubt"), ancient literature ("the grace of fable stirs the mind"), theology ("I revered our theology, and aspired as much as any one to reach heaven"), jurisprudence, medicine and other sciences that "secure for their cultivators honours and riches," (but, unfortunately, not true knowledge) as well as rhetoric and poetry in which he, as he admits, "was in love." However, none of these gave him what he was looking for, i.e. "the certitude and evidence of their reasonings." Indeed, he only found this in mathematics, but at the time of his studies he did not possess "as yet a precise knowledge of their true use; and thinking that they but contributed to the advancement of the mechanical arts."

Descartes weaved all these critical comments on the different sciences and those practicing them with tips on what to look for in the sciences, how to look for it, and what is useful in the search. As to this last element, Descartes points to human reason. At times it is the same as common sense, and at other times it is contrasted to it; yet in these preliminary considerations, this contrast is of no huge importance (that is, the negation of the cognitive abilities of common sense). What is more important is that "everyone thinks himself so abundantly provided with [common sense], that those even who are the most difficult to satisfy in everything else, do not usually desire a larger measure of this quality

---

[3] E. Husserl takes on a similar approach in his *Cartesian Meditations*. In the introduction to his work, he states that "Descartes, in fact, inaugurates an entirely new kind of philosophy. Changing its total style, philosophy takes a radical turn: from naive Objectivism to transcendental subjectivism which, with its ever new but always inadequate attempts, seems to be striving toward some necessary final form, wherein its true sense and that of the radical transmutation itself might become disclosed." Cf. E. Husserl, *Cartesian Meditations*, The Hague 1982, p. 4.

[4] "And yet I was studying in one of the most celebrated schools in Europe, in which I thought there must be learned men, if such were anywhere to be found." Cf. Descartes, *Discourse on the Method*, New York 2008, p. 12.

than they already possess." It is important to add that what is necessary in this quest is a set of rules – because rules are exactly what allowed him to form a "method that gives me the means, as I think, of gradually augmenting my knowledge, and of raising it by little and little to the highest point which the mediocrity of my talents and the brief duration of my life will permit me to reach." Everything in this short sentence is important – from the indication of the need of "a method" (let us add: an infallible one), through the words "as I think" (forming a certain protection), to the indication of the need for "gradually augmenting my knowledge, and of raising it by little and little to the highest point."

Further, it appears that this highest level achievable by the human mind is a cognition that is absolutely certain and absolutely true. Obviousness is considered to be the sign of certainty (which is such a state of mind in which no longer any reasons for doubt arise). Clarity and explicitness are considered to be the signs of truth. Descartes points to the necessity of such treating of these signs and using them in cognitive practice both in his *Rules for the Direction of the Mind*, and in the *Principles of Philosophy*.[5] Meanwhile, indications appearing in the *Discourse on the Method* and connected with this question may be treated as first-degree approximations to the problem of there being reliable evidence of certainty and truthfulness. However, even these can be regarded as such only up to the point where the human mind exceeds the threshold of seeking a reliable method of cognition (and wandering over a space of multiple unknowns) and does not set foot on the solid ground of those reasons whose certainty and truth can no longer beat all doubted; and if someone casts any doubt on them, it can be proven that these doubts are groundless.

This is one of the elements of the peculiar cognitive strategy adopted and used by Descartes, a strategy that in part three of the *Discourse on the Method* is called the "provisory code of morals." Among other things, it also allows the use of metaphor (such as comparing this provision to residing in a temporary house), recognition and application in the practice of what others recognize and use (provided, however, that these are the "laws, customs and views of the most reasonable of people"), and require, among other things, "conduct in every other matter according to the most moderate opinions, and the farthest removed from extremes," "to be as firm and resolute in my actions as I was able" and "not to adhere less steadfastly to the most doubtful opinions" and "to conquer myself rather than fortune," and to "accustom myself to the

---

[5] Cf. Descartes, *Rules for the Direction of the Mind*, in: *The philosophical writings of Descartes*, vol. 1, Cambridge 1985, p. 9 ff.; Descartes, *Principles of Philosophy*, in: *The philosophical writings of Descartes*, vol. 1, p. 190. For more on the subject, see: Z. Drozdowicz, *Kartezjusz a współczesność*, Poznan 1980, p. 58 ff.

persuasion that, except our own thoughts, there is nothing absolutely in our power."[6] Each of these statements bears its own significance. But at the beginning of this great journey that is aiming towards truth and approaching it by smaller or bigger steps, it would be difficult to fully explain its importance to the ones who are travelling, and why exactly it is this that is of importance and not any other. Therefore, what remains is to convince them that in fact there is (both because of the "mediocrity of mind" and because of the length of the "journey") no choice other than to rely on a good guide, and that this guide may be just the one who at least once has reached the destination. Of course, the aim is to achieve absolute certainty and absolute truth, or – which is really the same thing – true knowledge. Obviously, Descartes is convinced that he meets this condition, and the whole difficulty lies in convincing the reader of the *Discourse on the Method* about it too.

Although this is not the only goal of the *Discourse*, its realization determines the realization of all the other goals. Therefore Descartes chooses his words so carefully in order to encourage the reader of this dissertation to follow him and not be discouraged. Among other things, to this purpose he makes declarations (and certain mystifications) that "he has never imagined that his mind was more perfect in anything than average minds," and his thought was "equally brilliant, his imagination equally bright and memory so retentive and conscious as that of some other people" and also that "he only accidentally found himself on the roads that led him to certain considerations and principles." However, we must add that this kind of declarations (and mystifications) have their reason solely on the grounds of the Cartesian method of persuading the truth to others, or leading others to it. But they do not have and cannot have their reasons on the grounds of the Cartesian method of discovering it by oneself and the Cartesian method of justifying truth. In short, that which belongs to the Cartesian standard of the rationality of convincing one of the truth does not and cannot belong to the Cartesian standards of the discovery and justification of the truth.

The latter standards are presented in a general outline in the *Discourse on the Method*. They are discussed mainly in the second part of this dissertation. In the beginning, there again appears the Cartesian *vote of separation* from such a "treasure trove of knowledge," which is "knowledge" taken from books. Descartes does not trust this knowledge as "the sciences contained in books (such of them at least as are made up of probable reasonings, without demonstrations), composed as they are of the opinions of many different individuals massed together, are [...] removed from truth." Then there is quite a general indication of "the simple inferences which a man of good sense using his natural and

---

[6] Cf. Descartes, *Discourse on the method*, op. cit., p. 24.

unprejudiced judgment draws respecting the matters of his experience."[7] Further on he writes about a conditional suspension of trust "to any opinions" – so as "to recognise it later as true or other more accurate views, or the same ones if only I would manage to adapt them to the requirements of reason." Let us add – one's own individual reason. Although neither in this part nor in the further parts of the *Discourse on the Method* will we find an answer to the question about what kind of reason is that human cognitive power to which one can and must have complete confidence, at least we learn so much as there are two different kinds of reason (mind) – one willing to "precipitate in their judgments and want the patience requisite for orderly and circumspect thinking" and the other as "take the liberty to doubt of their accustomed opinions, and quit the beaten highway, they will never be able to thread the byway that would lead them by a shorter course." Of course, the latter is the Cartesian mind. In the *Rules for the Direction of the Mind* it is called intellect and presented as "a pure and careful mind." It is combined there with intellectual intuition, also known as the "light of reason" ("pure and careful").[8] In the light of the arguments contained in Descartes' dissertation, every man has such a mind and such a light. But the art of rational thinking does not consist in only possessing them, but rather in using them properly, and of this only few are capable.

The answer to the question of how intelligence should be used in discovering truth is contained in four Cartesian rules – the first one recommends "never to accept anything for true which I did not clearly know to be such," the second, "to divide each of the difficulties under examination into as many parts as possible, and as might be necessary for its adequate solution," the third, "to conduct my thoughts in such order that, by commencing with objects the simplest and easiest to know, I might ascend by little and little, and, as it were, step by step, to the knowledge of the more complex;" [...] and the last, "in every case to make enumerations so complete, and reviews so general, that I might be assured that nothing was omitted."[9] It is worth noting that the outline of these rules was preceded by the principle of reductionism – in this case it manifests itself in reducing "the great number of precepts of which logic is composed" to four. This reductionism is also part of the Cartesian standards of discovering truth, its justification and of convincing others to follow it.

Cartesian standards of rationality look differently in his *Meditations on First Philosophy*; although here too there is a variation depending on whether what is concerned is convincing one of the truth, its discovery or its justification;

    [7] Cf. ibidem, p. 18. In the original French text, Descartes writes about someone who uses common sense (un homme de bon sens).

    [8] Cf. Descartes, *Rules for the Direction of the Mind*, op. cit., p. 25 ff.

    [9] Cf. Descartes, *Discourse on the method*, op. cit., p. 21.

in any case, they are treated with greater intellectual rigor than in the *Discourse on the Method*. In *Meditations*, the use of common sense, biography, or history is reduced to a minimum. Although there still are references to metaphor, it is used quite moderately, bearing in mind that the human intellect, which is the focus of *Meditations*, feels best not in metaphorical ambiguity, but rather in mathematical unambiguity. This is probably why Descartes, in his description of the construction of a philosophical system, clearly restrains himself in comparing such a system to erecting a house – even though such a comparison is justified; *Meditation I*, is nothing else than "pulling down an old house" while the chapters that follow (six, in sum), are nothing other than a construction of subsequent levels on the solid grounds which survived the destructive power of the intellect.

However, one can also do without this metaphor and say generally that the *Meditations* are the exposition of the philosophy of principles, and these principles (to use Husserl's terminology) are a programme of:

– anti-naturalism, expressed in the opposition to everything that looks for support in the natural(material, sensual) world.

– anti-psychologism, expressed in the opposition to everything that is based on more or less clearly articulated psychological relationships (associations, feelings, etc.).

– anti-historicism, expressed in the opposition to everything that looks for and finds justification for its ideas in more or less clearly articulated experiences of past generations.

All this belongs to those Cartesian negations which answer the question asked in the title of *Meditation I*: "Of the Things of Which You May Doubt", and its essential complement in the form of questions: "Why do you doubt these things?" and "Why not doubt for the sake of doubting itself?" Descartes' response to the second of these questions is that you can only doubt that which "has the appropriate reasons," and "doubt only that [one] may doubt", which is an imitation of those Skeptics who simply multiply the uncertainty, and hence, do not seek truth, nor even agree that accessing truth is possible. However, the whole Cartesian "design was singly to find grounds of assurance, and cast aside the loose earth and sand" (this metaphor is quoted after the *Discourse on the Method*). Therefore, it does not have and cannot have anything to do with the actions of the Skeptics, and ascribing some versions of scepticism (called "methodical scepticism") to Descartes is one of the main misunderstandings staining various presentations of his views.[10]

---

[10] This scepticism comes down to Descartes's discovery of absolutely certain and absolutely true knowledge as well as to "the doubtfulness (of falseness) of all cognition, only in order to demonstrate with the appropriate proof that not everything could be doubted without a paradox. That which is doubtless is self-consciousness which, for Descartes, is

His views do, however, have a lot in common with an approach that, at least since Kant, has been commonly associated with rational criticism. A hallmark of criticism, with its complimentary self-criticism, is a specific rule and recommendation presented at the beginning of *Meditation I*, stating that one should approach everything *cautiously* and "no less scrupulously withhold one's assent from what is not fully certain and indubitable than from what is blatantly false."[11] This rule is immediately supplemented with another rule and recommendation: to search for reasons in everything; one reason would be enough to consider something untrue; however, to recognize something as true, only one reason would not be enough.

How the application of these principles looks in practice is illustrated by the subsequent steps in cognition taken by Descartes in his *Meditations*. In their light, it appears that one can and should reasonably doubt the credibility of what is communicated to us by the senses. For such doubting a far-reaching criticism is not necessary, and neither is a far-reaching self-criticism. Indeed the senses many a time are proved to be unreliable, and "prudence requires never to trust completely those who have deceived us even once." A certain amount of criticism and self-criticism is needed here, among other things, to prevent exaggeration and not to allow contesting of the fact that this external world exists at all. At first Descartes called the people questioning this fact crazy. However, after a deeper reflection, he concludes that they may in fact be right. The reason behind this might be, for example, taking a dream for reality: for how often does a dream make one think that "I'm here, I'm wearing my clothes, I was sitting by the fire, while actually I am lying undressed in bed."

In the next step, Descartes shows that one can reasonably doubt also that which is suggested to us by the imagination, for example, "the sirens and satyrs in the most extraordinary characters." Criticism inclines us here to doubt, while self-criticism to refrain from doubting that the creations of the imagination are merely a random composition of different things or states existing in reality – for example, "although these general objects, viz. [a body], eyes, a head, hands, and the like, [are] imaginary, we are nevertheless absolutely necessitated to admit the reality at least of some other objects still more simple and universal than these, of which, just as of certain real colours, all those images of things, whether true and real, or false and fantastic, that are found in our consciousness are formed."[12]

---

the hallmark of his philosophy." Cf. W. Augustyn, *Podstawy wiedzy u Descartes'a i Malebranche'a*, Warsaw 1973, p. 14 ff.

[11] Cf. Descartes, *Meditations on First Philosophy*, Oxford 2008, p. 17.

[12] Cf. ibidem, p. 15.

And the next step in cognition is to deepen the Cartesian criticism and self-criticism. It turns out that one can reasonably doubt not only the infallibility of the senses and imagination, but he can also doubt the reliability of the intellect, a thing that was, up to this point, most trustworthy. The reason compelling us to doubt it is the assumption that "some evil spirit, supremely powerful and cunning, has devoted all his efforts to deceiving me." This supposition evokes a criticism which leads to believing that this "evil spirit" can never make "me be nothing as long as I think that I am something." (I exist) if only to be deceived, and I exist as a thinking thing (*res cogitans*). "So that, having weighed all these considerations sufficiently and more than sufficiently, I can finally decide that this proposition, "I am, I exist" must be true whenever it is uttered by me, or conceived in the mind," and it remains true, as long as I think, or understand something with my mind. But there is also self-criticism and the question it bears: "But what therefore am I? A thinking thing? What is that? I mean a thing that doubts, that understands, that affirms, that denies, that wishes to do this and does not wish to do that, and also that imagines and perceives by the senses. Well, indeed, there is quite a lot there, if all these things really do belong to me. But why should they not belong to me? Is it not me who currently doubts virtually everything, who nonetheless understands something..." etc.

Certainly, this series of questions could go on since all of the Cartesian cognitive steps are accompanied by criticism and self-criticism, providing every statement with question marks, and leaving them until the last of the reasons for doubt is repealed. This process is, however, based on the general principles adopted and practiced by Descartes. These general principles come down to two, namely to the hypothetic-deductive principle on the discovery of truths and the axiomatic-deductive principle of justifying them. From this perspective, in *Meditations on First Philosophy* we can distinguish the three basic steps for the construction of arguments and evidence. The starting point for the first one forming a hypothesis: if "I" think about anything, therefore "I" necessarily exist. The positive solution of this hypothesis gives a premise (treated as an axiom) to pose another hypothesis: if "I" I think about myself and "about God" then "God" necessarily exists. The positive solution of this hypothesis gives a premise (also treated as an axiom) to make a hypothesis: if "I" think about myself, about "God" and "material (carnal) things" then these things necessarily exist, and I am certain of their existence, as long as I think about them and in this thinking I use my intellect properly, i.e., in the Cartesian manner. Thus, we return to the starting point. The latter obviously is not the *cogito ergo sum* formula, but the use of the intellect and confidence in its cognitive abilities.

Therefore, it can be said that Cartesian philosophy with the standards of rationality formulated on its grounds, in the final analysis is not a philosophy of negation, but that of affirmation, or to be more precise, an affirmation philosophy whose program contains:

– intellectualism, expressed, among other things, in the recognition of the human intellect as the only trustworthy cognitive authority, and in the use of its cognitive power in all situations where you must ultimately provide a "yes" or "no" answer;

– logicism, expressed, among other things, in the consistent adherence to accepted cognitive standards and the principles of logical thinking;

– deductive maximalism, expressed in such thinking that allows the derivation of as many consequences as possible from basic assumptions, adopted and treated as axioms, and postulating the possibility of further assumptions.

This reading of Cartesian affirmations, along with the Cartesian negations presented above, proves that – to quote E. Husserl – "Descartes, in fact, inaugurates an entirely new kind of philosophy. Changing its total style, philosophy takes a radical turn: from naive Objectivism" (read: naturalism) "to transcendental subjectivism" (read: intellectualism).

Quite an extensive body of work has been devoted to illustrating this Cartesian struggle to free the meditating individual from this "naivety" and to strengthen this individual's "subjectivism." There is no need to recall them here. Therefore, I will say briefly: they present different opinions, both in terms of the sensibleness (rationality) of undertaking this struggle, and in terms of how it should be conducted and of its final outcome. One such attempt at depreciating Cartesianism was *The Objections and Replies* submitted to the first edition of *Meditations* and published together with the dissertation, along with the replies from the author. What dominates it is the general conviction that the intellectual battle undertaken by Descartes ended in failure. According to some of his opponents (e.g., P. Gassendi, author of *Fifth Replies*), it could not have been successful because Descartes's posing such a pseudo-problem as the question of the existence of the corporeal world (extensible things) had to lead to such pseudo-solutions, such as the issue of the existence of the soul, which, being located, in the pineal gland (an endocrine gland located between the two hemispheres of the brain) in fact does not exist (as *res cogitans* it does not and cannot occupy any space).[13]

Of course, not all the arguments formulated in these and other objections to the *Meditations* have preserved their topicality until our times. What remains topical is the question that is repeated in them and concerns the solidity of the "bridge" erected by Descartes between the world of thought (*res cogitans*) and the world of corporeal things (*res extensa*). Without a doubt, the philosopher

---

[13] Cf. P. Gassendi, *Fifth Replies*, in: Descartes, *Meditations on First Philosophy*, op. cit., p. 183.

made an attempt to build such a bridge, and was convinced that the standards of rationality proposed by him served both as reliable pillars for this bridge as well as provided a completely secure passage from one side to the other.

2. Immanuel Kant

Immanuel Kant (1724-1804) is a philosopher of such magnitude that calling him a Cartesian scholar may raise some doubts among experts on his philosophy. Such identification, however, appears in the subject literature and it is not groundless.[14] However, we must add that Kant's philosophy was not a simple continuation of the standards of rationality that had been adopted and implemented by Descartes. Arguments supporting this claim are found in, among other things, the references to Cartesian standards which appear in Kant's dissertations. In his *Critique of Pure Reason* the name of his great predecessor appears several times and in each case it is accompanied by critical comments. For example, in the summary of the arguments contained in the first volume of this work, Descartes is presented as a representative of "material idealism" in its "problematic" version, i.e., one in which there is "the undoubted certainty of only one empirical assertion" (assertio), to wit, "I am." This "problematic idealism" is contrasted by Kant with "the dogmatic idealism of Berkeley" – in the latter it is assumed that space is "a property, which belongs to things in themselves" ("in that case it is, with all to which it serves as condition, a nonentity"). Although "problematic idealism" assumes nothing of this kind, still it "alleges our incapacity to prove the existence of anything besides ourselves by means of immediate experience," which indeed is evidence of "thorough philosophical thinking." However, it contains an internal contradiction ("internal and, to Descartes, indubitable experience is itself possible only under the previous assumption of external experience," which this philosopher considered doubtful). This is just one of those Cartesian solutions that Kant considered to be irrational.

The answer to the question of which idealism was in Kant's opinion non-problematic requires a closer look at Kantian affirmations and negations. Therefore, let us note at the beginning that this philosopher introduced into philosophy a distinction between the pre-critical rationalism and the critical rationalism. He was ready to accept the general formulas of the former until 1755, that is, until the publication of the dissertation *A New Explanation of the First Principles of Metaphysical Knowledge*. The appearance in the title of this work

---

[14] Cf., for example, B. Paź, *Naczelna zasada racjonalizmu. Od Kartezjusza do wczesnego Kanta*, Cracow 2007, p. 404 ff.

of the concept of "principle" indicates that its author wished to remain within the traditional philosophy of the principles – in particular the Wolffian one. He studies it because he needed it for the lectures on metaphysics, which he delivered at Königsberg University. According to B. Paź, Kant found in Wolff's philosophy, most of all, logicisation, i.e., firstly, bringing major philosophical problems down to cognitive issues, and secondly, the cognitive problems of logic.[15] An expression of this logicisation in the pre-critical Kant is also the recognition, first that: "There are two absolutely primary principles of all truths, one of them is the principle of affirmative truths, namely a theorem: whatever is, is, and the second one is the principle of negative truths, namely a statement: whatever is not, is not. Both these statements at the same time are given the same name of the principle of identity"; second, that the guiding principle of rationalism is the principle of identity, not that of contradiction ("We must ensure the primacy of the principle of identity over the principle of contradiction to establish a guiding principle in the order of truths"). For these assumptions, Kant gave a thorough logical justification, which can also be regarded as a peculiar expression of his logicisation. It results from this that we can and should speak reasonably of two complementary types of rationality, i.e. the rationality of affirmations (affirmative proposition) and the rationality of negation, the refutation ("it is a negative proposition").

This issue is the starting point in his *Critique of Pure Reason* (1781), a work which, like the *Critique of Practical Reason* (1788) and the *Critique of the Power of Judgment* (1790), presents an interpretation of Kantian critical rationalism. In the *Preface* to the first edition Kant states that "human reason, in one sphere of its cognition, is called upon to consider questions, which it cannot decline, as they are presented by its own nature, but which it cannot answer, as they transcend every fault of the mind. It falls into this difficulty without any fault of its own. It begins with principles, which cannot be dispensed with in the field of experience, and the truth and sufficiency of which are, at the same time, insured by experience."[16] This can be seen as a justification typical of the Enlightenment thinkers or as an excuse by human nature to the rationality of affirmation and to the rationality of negation.

In the further part of the *Preface*, however, there appears a Kantian *vote of separation* from the traditional (read: under-critical) affirmation and negation. Kant calls the representatives of the former the "dogmatists" and enumerates various kinds of their "sins" (such as "despotic dominion" in the old days, or unjustified claims to put an end to all the disputes in his times); he calls the

---

[15] Cf. ibidem, p. 356 ff.
[16] Cf. I. Kant, *Critique of Pure Reason*, New York 2004, p. xix.

representatives of the latter the "skeptics" – they, in turn, have to account for such "achievements" as bringing about "complete anarchy" in antiquity and, in modern times, bringing "complete indifferentism" ("the father of chaos and night"). To both these options he opposes the standpoint of critical rationalism, i.e., one where reason undertakes again "the most laborious of all tasks – that of self-examination and [establishing] a tribunal, which may secure it in it its well-grounded claims [...] This tribunal is nothing less than the critical investigation of pure reason. I do not mean by this a criticism of books and systems (as many Enlightenment philosophers did – A/N), but a critical inquiry into the faculty of reason, with reference to the cognitions to which it strives to attain without the aid of experience; in other words, the solution may secure it in its well-grounded question regarding the possibility or impossibility of metaphysics, and the determination of the origin, as well as of the extent and limits of this science. All this must be done on the basis of principles."[17]

In the preface to the second edition of the *Critique of Pure Reason* (1787) such a definition of the rational (reasonable) goal of criticism was called by him "the Copernican Revolution" – because what he proposed was "just what Copernicus did in attempting to explain the celestial movements. When he found that he could make no progress by assuming that all the heavenly bodies revolved round the spectator, he reversed the process, and tried the experiment of assuming that the spectator revolved, while the stars remained at rest. We may make the same experiment with regard to the intuition of objects, if the intuition must conform to the nature of the objects, I do not see how we can know anything of them *a priori*. If, on the other hand, the object conforms to the nature of our faculty of intuition, I can then easily conceive the possibility of such an *a priori* knowledge."[18] This "Copernican Sun" or – which is just the same thing – the guiding principle, however, is not, in Kant's view, the so-called "pure reason"; although he states that "Pure reason is a perfect unity; and therefore, if the principle presented by it prove to be insufficient for the solution of even a single one of those questions to which the very nature of reason gives birth, we must reject it." Then it turns out that the emphasis is put on *a priori* knowledge ["to furnish the standard – and consequently an example of all apodictic (philosophical) certitude"] and also on that which makes it possible, and it is to be made possible by the transcendental elements of human cognition, i.e. such which – as component parts of the recognizing subject – determine this cognition, but are not conditioned by that which is being recognized. Thus, it can be assumed that the guiding principle of

---

[17] Cf. ibidem, p. xxi.
[18] Cf. ibidem, p. xxxii.

Kantian rationalism is the principle of transcendentalism. In favour of such a standpoint also speaks the fact that Kant gave his *Critique of Pure Reason* the subtitle: *Transcendental Science of Elements.*

In the Introduction, he explains that "transcendental philosophy is the idea of a science, for which the Critique of Pure Reason must sketch the whole plan architectonically, that is, from principles, with a full guarantee for the vitality and stability of all the parts which enter into the building. It is the system of all the principles of pure reason. If this Critique itself does not assume the title of transcendental philosophy, it is only because, to be a complete system, it ought to contain a full analysis of all human knowledge a priori." A little further he adds that this "full analysis" is carried out only in so far as is needed to fully assess the "synthetic *a priori* knowledge."[19] Previously, he explained what a "synthetic *a priori* knowledge" is. Both these explanations, as well as the following part of Kantian reasoning, serve to convince that we are dealing with an equality sign between the philosophical (or, in Kantian terminology: "metaphysical") rationalism and a strict – which is just the same thing – apodeictic logicalism, i.e., such in which there is no room left for any contingent cognitive solutions. In short, the logic of Kantian pure reason is the logic of "either or", i.e. it does not allow the slightest deviation from any of the principles (rules). Components of this logicalism are the transcendental aesthetics and transcendental logic. Within the latter Kant distinguished transcendental analytics and transcendental dialectics. With his characteristic precision, or – as his biographers say – pedantry, in the *Introduction* to the *Critique of Pure Reason* he gave his rationalisation (reasons) for this division.[20]

In Kantian terms, transcendental aesthetics is "the science of all the principles of sensibility a priori." The term 'transcendental' means here that it deals with what "is a condition under which objects are given to us," sensory, or – which is just the same thing – that which constitutes "pure"

---

[19] In the light of this explanation, this is a knowledge whose result is formulating synthetic *a priori* judgments, that is, determining sentences in which the relation of subject A to predicate B is such that "the predicate B is completely out of the conception A, although it stands in connection with it;" a judgment in which "the predicate B belongs to the subject A, as somewhat which is contained (though covertly) in the conception A" is called analytical. The term *a priori* means knowledge which "is independent of this or that kind of experience, but such as is absolutely so of all experience. Opposed to this is empirical knowledge, or that which is possible only a posteriori, that is, through experience." Cf. ibidem, p. xlvii.

[20] In its light, he bases on the assumption that "there are two cores of human cognition which, perhaps, stem from one, unknown to us, common core, that is, sensuality and intellect. Through the first, objects are given to us, through the second, they are thought of." On the subject of Kant's personality, and on his "pedantry", see: W. Weischedel, *Die philosophische Hintertreppe. Die grossen Philosophen in Alltag und Denken*, Munich 1973, p. 177 ff.

forms of sensory perception; we call "pure (in the transcendental sense) any representation, in which there is nothing, which would be an impression." It turns out that these forms are space and time. Kant says that the former "is not an empirical concept," but is "a necessary representation a priori, which serves for the foundations of all external intuitions. [...] It must, therefore, be considered as the condition of the possibility of phenomena, and by no means as a determination dependent on them..." It is similar with time, which from the point of view of transcendental aesthetics is "is given a priori. In it alone is all reality of phenomena possible. These may all be annihilated in thought, but time itself, as the universal condition of their possibility, cannot be so annulled." Among other things, it means that, unlike the phenomena, which may be accidental, occasional and dependent, space and time are necessary, universal and independent of what is currently the subject of cognition; it is not and cannot be dependent on it, because "one cannot assign objects to themselves (apart from their relation to our viewing) or as something which would be in them an object of property or as something which would belong to them as a feature." To put it briefly, space and time belong to the cognitive equipment of every human being – on the same basis as the five basic senses of cognition belong to him as well. The latter are called by Kant the "external senses", while the former, the internal ones. By their means "the mind sees itself and its internal condition," which means that indeed they are not a part of the mind (intellect), but they perform specific cognitive functions for it.

Forms of mental cognition are the subject of Kantian transcendental logic. Due to the difference between general objectives, Kant distinguishes "the logic of the general use of understanding", and "the logic of its particular application." "The first contains the absolutely necessary laws of thought, without which no use whatsoever of the understanding is possible. [...] The logic of the particular use of the understanding contains the laws of correct thinking upon a particular class of objects." In the former, which is also called "pure logic", "we abstract all the empirical conditions under which the understanding is exercised; for example, the influence of the senses, the play of the fantasy or imagination, the laws of the memory, the force of habit, of inclination, etc. [...] General logic is called applied, when it is directed to the laws of the use of the understanding, under the subjective empirical conditions which psychology teaches us. It has therefore empirical principles, although, at the same time, it is in so far general, that it applies to the exercise of the understanding, without regard to the difference of objects without regard to the difference of objects." When explaining the sense of the use of the term "transcendental" in relation to logic, Kant states that it is a science, which "deals exclusively with the laws of intellect and reason, but only insofar as they are related objects *a priori*."

Following these explanations, Kant introduced the division of general logic into analytics and dialectics. The first of these "breaks all the formal activities of intellect and reason into its ultimate constituents and presents them as guiding principles of any assessment of our knowledge." "That part of transcendental logic, then, which treats of the elements of pure cognition of the understanding, and of the principles without which no object at all can be thought, is transcendental analytic, and at the same time a logic of truth." These elements appear to be "pure concepts of the intellect," which Kant also called the categories. He lists four groups of such concepts, distinguishing three categories in each of them. In total, this gives twelve categories.[21] About each of them the same thing can be said as about space and time, i.e., that it has a transcendental character, that it is a prerequisite to cognition (in this case, an intellectual one), without being conditioned by its object. To the question: Where do these concepts come from?, Kant replies that they "spring pure and unmixed out of the understanding as an absolute unity."

The main goal of transcendental logic, however, is not to split thought into elements or components, but to achieve a logical synthesis of "various a priori data." This activity of the mind consists, according to Kant, in "joining different representations to each other and of comprehending their diversity in one cognition. This synthesis is pure when the diversity is not given empirically but a priori (as that in space and time). Our representations must be given previously to any analysis of them; and no conceptions can arise, [in respect to] their content, analytically. But the synthesis of a diversity (be it given a priori or empirically) is the first requisite for the production of a cognition, which in its beginning, indeed, may be crude and confused, and therefore in need of analysis..." Further he explains that "to reduce this synthesis to conceptions is a function of the understanding." However, it turns out even further that there are more such functions performed by the understanding within the transcendental analytics. Among others, there is the discovery of "the main principles of transcendental deduction in general," and the discovery of "a system of all principles of pure understanding", while "the supreme principle of all analytical judgments," turns out to be the principle of contradiction ("To none of the things belongs a feature that would contradict it" is called by him "the principle of contradiction").[22]

---

[21] "How did Kant arrive at this number? He referred to logic, in which he found a division of judgments in terms of quantity, quality, and modality. Each of these divisions he separated further into three sub-groups, and added one group for their relations (categorical, hypothetical, and disjunctive imperative). He therefore arrived at twelve judgments and twelve respective categories." Cf. T. Kroński, *Kant*, Warsaw 1966, p. 22 ff.

[22] "The result of the whole of this part of the analytic of principles is, therefore that: "All principles of the pure understanding are nothing more than a priori principles of the

In the conclusion to this presentation of transcendental analytics, Kant characterizes the area of the power of pure reason as a land in which the intellect cannot only "carefully [survey] every part of it, but [is able to do] it, and [assign] to everything therein its proper place. But this land is an island, and enclosed by nature herself within unchangeable limits. It is the land of truth (an attractive word), surrounded by a wide and stormy ocean, the region of illusion, where many a fog-bank, many an iceberg, seems to the mariner, on his voyage of discovery, a new country, and, while constantly deluding him with vain hopes, engages him in dangerous adventures, from which he never can desist, and which yet he never can bring to termination." This is a metaphor – something that relatively rarely appears in the work of a philosopher whose ambition was to precisely say everything that can and needs to be said to stay within the limits of rationality. Kant's use of this metaphor, however, is here deeply justified. It is because he came to an extreme situation; namely, one in which intellectual criticism must be supplemented with self-criticism, i.e. a cognitive approach, which will allow not only to become aware of intellectual capabilities, but also intellectual impossibility, including the impossibility of making a bridge between the world of phenomena (occurrences) and, at the same time, entering the world of noumena (things in themselves) with a firm step.[23]

Kantian transcendental dialectics deals with this cognitively impassable boundary between the two worlds. As in the case of transcendental analytics, its overall aim is to achieve a logical synthesis of the various elements of intellectual cognition, but – in contrast to the former – what is meant here is a global synthesis, or – which is just the same – the synthesis of "the ultimate constituents" of this cognition. On the way to this synthesis, a critical and self-critical intellect must, among other things, cope with various kinds of:

– "illusory appearance" such as "illogical illusion, which consists merely in the imitation of the form of reason;"

– "paralogisms of pure reason," such as "logical paralogism" ("The logical paralogism consists in the falsity of an argument in respect of its form, be the content what it may") or "substantiality paralogism" (an example of this is the Cartesian formula, "cogito ergo sum");

---

possibility of experience, and to experience alone do all a priori synthetical propositions apply and relate" Cf. ibidem, p. 161.

[23] "The possibility of a thing can never be proved from the fact that the conception of it is not self contradictory, but only by means of an intuition corresponding to the conception. If, therefore, we wish to apply the categories to objects which cannot be regarded as phenomena, we must have an intuition different from the sensuous, and in this case the objects would be a noumena in the positive sense of the word." Cf. ibidem, p. 169.

– and antinomies, among others, such as appear "in the system of cosmological ideas;" according to Kant, one of them is the antinomy between the thesis that "The world has a beginning in time, and is also limited in regard of space," and its antithesis that "The world has no beginning, and no limits in space, but is, in relation both to time and space, infinite."[24]

The comprehensive Volume II of the *Critique of Pure Reason* is largely devoted to the criticism of these standpoints, in which these appearances are taken for reality, paralogisms are taken for logicity and antinomies for logical consistency. About those who advocate such standpoints, Kant wrote that they use "various juggling tricks" and "sophistical delusions." Criticism and self-criticism, which is an element of Kantian transcendental dialectics – apart from everything else – "has the task of exposing the groundless nature of the pretensions of these two faculties, and invalidate their claims to the discovery and enlargement of our cognitions merely by means of transcendental principles, and show that the proper employment of these faculties is to test the judgements made by the pure understanding, and to guard it from sophistical delusion." In practice it turns out to be equivalent to:

– First, the recognition of the irrational speculative psychology ("the science" of the human soul), theology ("the science" of the divine being), and cosmology ("the science" of the beginning and end of the world, its borders or its infinitude, etc.)

– Second, the discovery of a priori principles of transcendental psychology, theology and cosmology.

The first of these is the principle of ideals – ideals in general, and ideals, in particular, or – which is just the same – in their practical applications. They are supposed to be located – like the forms of sensory perception and the forms of the intellectual view – in the reason itself; "human reason contains not only ideas, but ideals, which possess, not, like those of Plato, creative, but certainly practical power – as regulative principles, and form the basis of the perfectibility of certain actions." Kant points to the existence in "pure reason" of three such ideals in particular (the regulatory principles), i.e., the unity of the subject, the unity of the object, and the unity of all subjects and objects. The basic function of these ideals is reduced to the introduction or preservation in cognition of "the greatest rational unity." When giving the reasons for the use of these ideals (the regulatory principles), he wrote that "guided by the principles involved in these ideas, we must, in the first place, so connect all the phenomena, actions, and feelings of the mind, as if it were a simple substance, which, endowed with personal identity, possesses a permanent existence (in this

---

[24] Cf. ibidem, p. 254.

life at least) [...]. Secondly, in cosmology, we must investigate the conditions of all natural phenomena, internal as well as external, as if they belonged to a chain infinite and without any prime or supreme member. [...] Thirdly, in the sphere of theology, we must regard the whole system of possible experience as forming an absolute, but dependent and sensuously conditioned unity, and at the same time as based upon a sole, supreme, and all-sufficient ground existing apart from the world itself – a ground which is a self-subsistent, primeval and creative reason, in relation to which we so employ our reason in the field of experience, as if all objects drew their origin from that archetype of all reason."[25] In the light of the *Critique of Pure Reason*, these "wishes," "pressures" and "considerations, as if" are and will remain reasonable as long as they are not entangled in assumptions, postulates and beliefs of the speculative reason, namely, that which celebrated its dubious success in the pre-critical period.

Based on these statements, a conclusion can be made that according to Kant, rational theology (the study of God) is, as a matter of fact, not possible just as psychology (the science of the soul) and cosmology (the science of the material world) are not possible.[26] Such a conclusion is justified only on the grounds of this version of rationalism, which was proclaimed by Kantian pure reason. However, it is not justified on the basis of Kantian rationalism created by practical reason. The evidence is contained in the *Critique of Practical Reason, Metaphysics of Morality, Justification of the Metaphysics of Morality*, i.e., the works in which Kant presented his second philosophy, assuming that his "first philosophy is the philosophy of pure reason."

With his characteristic precision, Kant answers the questions about the origin and purpose of this doubling of philosophy. In the introduction to the first of the above mentioned works, he makes it clear that in fact there is one reason, but that it has different uses, or areas of "dealing with problems". Reason is "pure" in its theoretical use when it "was concerned with objects of the cognitive faculty only, and a critical examination of it"; when "reason is concerned with the grounds of determination of the will, which is a faculty either to produce objects corresponding to ideas, or to determine ourselves to the effecting of such objects," then it is called "the practical reason." "Now, here there comes in a notion of causality justified by the critique of the pure reason, although not capable of being presented empirically, viz., that of freedom; and if we can now discover means of proving that this property does in fact belong to the human will (and so to the will of all rational beings), then it will not only be shown that pure reason can be practical, but that it alone, and

---

[25] Cf. ibidem, p. 408.

[26] The same conclusion is drawn in T. Kroński's monograph on Kant; cf. T. Kroński, *Kant*, op. cit., p. 30.

not reason empirically limited, is indubitably practical; consequently, we shall have to make a critical examination, not of pure practical reason, but only of practical reason generally. [...] The critique, then, of practical reason generally is bound to prevent the empirically conditioned reason from claiming exclusively to furnish the ground of determination of the will."[27]

The statements cited here show that although not everything is so clear as to leave no doubt, we can at least be certain that the subject of discussion in the *Critique of Practical Reason* is also a pure reason – only that here it is applied not to cognition but to human will, and that in it will also be included transcendental aspects (the faculty of will establishes a form of "transcendental freedom") and antinomies, or, more precisely, "the concept of causality in order to escape the antinomy into which [free will] inevitably falls". Therefore, it can be said that this work – like Kant's other writing in the field of moral philosophy – is aimed at indicating such a use for free will as to make it good ("moral" in the strict sense), and to use in accordance with the pure and the practical reason, or – as defined by Kant himself – "pure practical reason."[28]

What it is supposed to look like in detail is presented by this philosopher in the logic of practical reason, which, like the logic of pure reason, is divided – into the analytics and dialectics of "pure practical reason." The component parts of the first are: "practical principles" (these are "propositions which contain a general determination of the will"), "the concept of an object of pure practical reason" or "the idea of an object as an effect possible to be produced through freedom" and "moral law" ("what is essential in the moral worth of actions is that the moral law should directly determine the will") – this law is expressed by means of maxims, nevertheless they are of an obligatory character.[29]

In the last chapter of the analytics of "pure practical reason," devoted to its motives, or "the subjective grounds of determination of the will", Kant writes about the truth in these maxims. For this purpose he refers to the concept of "interest", which – in the light of these analytics – arises "from the notion of a motive [...], [and] which can never be attributed to any being unless it possesses reason, and which signifies a motive of the will in so far as it is conceived by the reason. Since in a morally good will the law itself must

---

[27] Cf. I. Kant, *Critique of Practical Reason*, New York 1954, p. 11.

[28] T. Kroński shares this understanding of these works – according to him "The *Critique of Practical Reason* investigates the factual conditions of "good will", tries to answer how it is possible that "good will", that is moral will, which must be undoubtedly existent, occurs in people in the first place, or, in other words, what are the conditions of the existence of pure morality." Cf. T. Kroński, *Kant*, op. cit., p. 32 ff.

[29] "The moral law is in fact for the will of a perfect being a law of holiness, but for the will of every finite rational being a law of duty, of moral constraint, and of the determination of its actions by respect for this law and reverence for its duty." Cf. ibidem, p. 70.

be the motive, the moral interest is a pure interest of practical reason alone, independent of sense. On the notion of an interest is based that of a maxim. This, therefore, is morally good only in case it rests simply on the interest taken in obedience to the law [...]. There is something so singular in the unbounded esteem for the pure moral law, apart from all advantage, as it is presented for our obedience by practical reason, the voice of which makes even the boldest sinner tremble and compels him to hide himself from it." A little further this voice is called "the voice of conscience," and its accusing power is considered to be so great that no one and nothing can silence it; unless, at the moment of committing a vile act, the individual "was not in his right mind, i.e., could not take advantage of his freedom." However, Kant did not want to deal extensively with such extraordinary or pathological situations, commenting on them briefly with a general statement that without the freedom of human will, "Man would be a marionette or an automaton, like Vaucanson's, prepared and wound up by the Supreme Artist."

In the dialectics of "pure practical reason", like in the analytics, Kant "seeks to find the unconditioned for the practically conditioned," yet not the "determinant of will" (as in moral law) is meant here, but rather "the unconditioned totality of the object of pure practical reason under the name of the *summum bonum*." In this search he encounters – just as in the dialectics of "only pure reason" – antinomies, in this case between happiness, which "must be the motive to maxims of virtue," and the maxim of virtue, which "must be the efficient cause of happiness." He removes this antimony (recognising that "the desire of personal happiness [is] not moral at all"), which allows him to reasonably adopt – first, "the primacy of pure practical reason" over the speculative reason, and second, such postulates of "pure practical reason" as "the postulate of immortality, the postulate of freedom [...] and the postulate of the existence of God."[30] He then moves on to reasons which aim at making these postulates apodeictic (exigent), and explains why they should be placed in the sphere of "pure practical reason" (as from the standpoint of pure reason itself, they are only hypotheses).

The book closes with the "Methodology" of pure practical reason, which forms a relatively small (only several pages long) Part II of the *Critique of Practical Reason*, the aim of which is to show "how we can give the laws of

---

[30] "The first results from the practically necessary condition of a duration adequate to the complete fulfillment of the moral law; the second from the necessary supposition of independence of the sensible world, and of the faculty of determining one's will according to the law of an intelligible world, that is, of freedom; the third from the necessary condition of the existence of the *summum bonum* in such an intelligible world, by the supposition of the supreme independent good, that is, the existence of God." Cf. ibidem, p. 102.

pure practical reason access to the human mind," and a two page conclusion which, among other things, contains that statement by Kant, which is sometimes quoted, that: "Two things fill the mind with ever new and increasing admiration and awe, the oftener and the more steadily we reflect on them: *the starry heavens above and the moral law within.*" In his commentary to this statement, Kant tries to convince the reader that what underlines this awe and admiration is not some intellectually incontrollable emotionalism, but, rather, a rigorous rationalism – which begins "from my invisible self, my personality, and exhibits me in a world which has true infinity, but which is traceable only by the understanding, and with which I discern that I am not in a merely contingent but in a universal and necessary connection."

To summarize, we can say that Kant has differentiated the standards of rationality – firstly, into standards of pre-critical philosophy and into standards of critical philosophy; secondly, in critical philosophy, into standards of pure reason and into standards of the pure practical reason. In each of these instances there are distinguishable subsequent standards, e.g. in the pre-critical philosophy, dogmatic and skeptical standards; in the critical philosophy, standards of the forms of sensory perception and standards of the forms of mental perception as well as the standards of regulatory ideas. What is problematic here is not only their precise distinction, but also their practical implementation, so that in the end we would be left only with that which has solid reasons supporting it. Certainly, this is the same problem which was considered by Descartes to be of primary importance. In this sense, Kant at the beginning and at the end of his philosophical journey towards rationality was, and remained, a Cartesian philosopher.

3. Georg Wilhelm Friedrich Hegel

According to experts on the history of philosophy, Georg Wilhelm Friedrich Hegel (1770-1831), and his philosophy, summarizes a certain stage in the rationalization of philosophical thinking. Herbert Schnädelbach claims that this philosophy concludes the process of a "demythologisation of reason," self-knowledge being its goal.[31] This great endeavour originated in the philosophy

---

[31] "'Demythologisation of reason' is a process in which reason loses its objective being-in- itself (Ansichsein) and is like all the mythical instances resolved to something exclusively human. This demythologisation of reason is an aspect of the dialectics of the Enlightenment. It was the Enlightenment, which always occurred under the sign of reason, which addresses critically against itself in its quasi-mythical figures. What happens after Hegel is nothing else than a manifestation that the dialectics of the Enlightenment now begin to encompass also

of Socrates. Let us recall that Hegel, in his *Lectures on the History of Philosophy*, presents Socrates as "the model of moral virtues": he is "a peaceful, pious example of moral virtues of wisdom, discretion, temperance, moderation, justice, courage, inflexibility, firm sense of rectitude to tyrants and people" – in short, a hero whose philosophical thinking and life "are carved from one solid piece," i.e. "a solid piece" of reason (rationality).[32] When trying to find the cause for the admiration of this ancient philosopher, Schnädelbach suggest that Hegel might have found in him "the dialectic of historical reason."[33] I am inclined to agree, and also to recognize that the standards of philosophical thought and conduct, postulated and applied by Hegel, are a part of this dialectic. The issue is, however, presented differently throughout Hegel's various works. An attempt at a comprehensive presentation of this dialectic and the related standards of rationality is contained in his *Science of Logic*, a work considered by the experts on his philosophy to be the "bible" of Hegelianism.[34] Therefore it is worth looking closer at the arguments contained therein.

Let us try to answer the question first, what, according to the intention of the philosopher, this logic is or should be? In the preface to the first edition of this work (published between 1812 and 1816) Hegel describes the reduction of logic into "teaching how to think" as "prejudice." However, in the Introduction to the book, he states that "When logic is taken as the science of thinking in general, it is understood that this thinking constitutes the *mere form* of a cognition that logic abstracts from all *content* and that the so-called second constituent belonging to cognition, namely its *matter*, must come from somewhere else; and that since this matter is absolutely independent of logic, this latter can provide only the formal conditions of genuine cognition and cannot in its own self contain any real truth, not even be the *pathway* to real truth."[35]

Of course, Hegel implies a logic which will contain the real truth, or at least will point to the path leading to it. This logic must combine the form of

---

the enlightened reason itself and threatens the ultimate leaving of it beyond itself. [...] Max Horkheimer tried to outline the history of the demythologisation of reason and the threat of its result, while he made a distinction between the objective and the subjective mind and – to put it simply – described the process of the subjectivisation of reason as the way to its full instrumentalisation." H. Schnädelbach, *Próba rehabilitacji animal rationale*, Warsaw 2001, p. 37 ff.

[32] Cf. G. W. F. Hegel, *Lectures on the History of Philosophy*, London 1892-1989, p. 452.

[33] Cf. H. Schnädelbach, *Rozum i historia*, Warsaw 1994, p. 60 ff.

[34] Cf. M. Siemek, *Hegel: Rozum i historia*, in: idem, *W kręgu filozofów*, Warsaw 1984, p. 41 ff. According to this historian, the leading thought of the *Science of Logic* comes down to the assumption (rationale) that "truth is a unity existing only in movement, only in the process of its self-becoming."

[35] Cf. G. W. F. Hegel, *Science of logic*, London 1969, p. 43. All the highlights in the quoted fragments come from Hegel.

cognition with its contents. This connection requires: first, the assumption that "the material of knowledge is present in and for itself as a ready-made world outside thinking", second, a "hierarchical relationship of these two components of knowledge" and third, observing in cognition of the difference between matter and form or making an assumption that "thinking therefore in its reception and formation of material does not go outside itself; its reception of the material and the conforming of itself to it remains a modification of its own self."

What follows are some critical remarks on the philosophical options, which in Hegel's view of reason and the Hegelian sense of rationality are either completely irrational or insufficiently rational – such as sensualism ("Turned against reason, this understanding behaves in the manner of *ordinary common sense*, giving credence to the latter's view that truth rests on sensuous reality"), or transcendental idealism, which "consistently conducted" indeed led to proving that "forms (of sensory and mental perception – A/N) *do not apply to things in themselves*", but "the subjective attitude assumed in the attempt prevented it from coming to fruition. This attitude and, together with it, the attempt and the cultivation of pure science were eventually abandoned" (this is a reference to Fichte and Schelling, among others). According to Hegel this was a mistake since that point "from which to start in science" (logic) is – in the language of Kant – "the realm of Pure Reason" ("*This realm is truth unveiled, truth as it is and for itself*"). Kant is considered by Hegel to be a great philosopher because "Kant had a higher regard for dialectic [...] for he removed from it the semblance of arbitrariness which it has in ordinary thought and presented it as *a necessary operation of reason.*"[36]

In the *Introduction* to the *Science of Logic*, among other things, Hegel refers to his *Phenomenology of Spirit,* published in 1807. In this work, he explains "the consciousness progresses from the first immediate opposition of itself and the subject matter to absolute knowledge" (that is, dialectical movement). We learn already from his *Preface* to the *Phenomenology of Spirit* that the eponymous spirit

---

[36] "The general idea on which he based his expositions and which he vindicated, is the objectivity of the illusion and the necessity of the contradiction which belongs to the nature of thought determinations: primarily, it is true, with the significance that these determinations are applied by reason to things in themselves; but their nature is precisely what they are in reason and with reference to what is intrinsic or in itself. This result, grasped in its positive aspect, is nothing else but the inner negativity of the determinations as their self-moving soul, the principle of all natural and spiritual life. [...] It is in this dialectic as it is here understood, that is, in the grasping of opposites in their unity or of the positive in the negative, that speculative thought consists. It is the most important aspect of dialectic, but for thinking which is as yet unpractised and unfree it is the most difficult." Cf. ibidem, p. 56.

"is never at rest but always engaged in moving forward."[37] Its march forward "interrupts graduation," but this is only a quantitative "break" in order to "gain strength" (like a "child after long, quiet nourishment") and "make a qualitative leap" toward the ever better (more rational) future. Hegel compares this march to "dissolving bit by bit of the structure of its previous world", and erecting in its place of new more complex parts, but also more intelligent ones, and the measure of this rationality is not so much the complexity itself of this new world, but the awareness of the builders of what this world is as the whole and in its parts. "Consciousness misses in the newly emerging shape its former range and specificity of content, and even more the articulation of form whereby distinctions are securely defined, and stand arrayed in their fixed relations."

However, all this appears after some time and not in a simple, but in a dialectical relation of "a lord and a bondsman." "The lord is the consciousness that exists *for itself*, but no longer merely the Notion of such a consciousness. Rather, it is a consciousness existing *for itself* which is mediated with itself through another consciousness, i.e. through a consciousness whose nature it is to be bound up with an existence that is independent, or thinghood in general. The lord puts himself into relation with both of these moments, to a *thing* as such, the object of desire, and to the consciousness for which thinghood is the essential characteristic [...] The Lord relates himself mediately to the bondsman through a being [a thing] that is independent, for it is just this which holds the bondsman in bondage; it is his chain from which he could not break free in the struggle, thus proving himself to be dependent, to possess his independence in thinghood. But the lord is the power over this thing, for he proved in the struggle that it is something merely negative [...] Equally, the lord relates himself mediately to the thing through the bondsman; the bondsman, *qua* self-consciousness in general, also relates himself negatively to the thing, and takes away its independence; but at the same time the thing is independent *vis-a-vis* the bondsman, whose negating of it, therefore, cannot go to the length of being altogether done with it to the point of annihilation; in other words, he only *works* on it. For the lord, on the other hand, the *immediate* relation becomes through this mediation the sheer negation of the thing, or the enjoyment of it." In this intellectually sophisticated Hegelian metaphor such important elements of his dialectics are contained: the enslavement through lower rationality (e.g. such as common-sense rationality) and liberation through the higher one and in the clash of opposing powers in the fighting of those which at a given stage of historical development appear to be more intelligent than those defeated.

---

[37] Cf. G. W. F. Hegel, *Phenomenology of Spirit*, Oxford 1977.

In the further parts of the *Phenomenology of Spirit* this bondage and the clashes between "master lord and bondsman" are presented on the basis of social life (the life of nations, governing, etc.), the impact of different cultural formations (such as "fighting with superstition during the Enlightenment"), and the clashes of different types of religion and religiosity (e.g., of the "religion of art" with "the open religion," and then of the latter with the "absolute religion"). In the last part of this work, Hegel shows the coming of that spirit to "absolute knowledge" ("This last shape of Spirit – the Spirit which at the same time gives its complete and true content the form of the Self and thereby realizes its Notion as remaining in its Notion in this realization – this is absolute knowing"), and its full self-knowledge. "It is Spirit that knows itself in the shape of Spirit, or a *comprehensive knowing* [in terms of the Notion]. Truth is not only *in itself* completely identical with certainty, but it also has the shape of self-certainty) or it is in its existence in the form of self-knowledge. [...] The nature, moments and movement of this knowing have, then, shown themselves to be such that this knowing is a pure *being-for-self* of self-consciousness." In this final moment of "the march of the spirit" all the "contradictions, oppositions, negativity shall be lifted", all "essentialities will be sucked" into one concept ("which is aware of itself as a concept"). "It is then that Spirit has grasped the Notion of itself, just as we now have first grasped it; and its shape or the element of its existence, being the Notion, is Spirit itself."[38]

The *Phenomenology of Spirit*, quoted here, is placed in the sphere of broadly understood ontological considerations. However, it contains several other motifs such as epistemological, ethical, historical, political ones, etc. Hegel's thought is global (holistic), and the diversity of the problems discussed in his dissertations results mainly from his endeavor to show some of the selected aspects or manifestations of one and the same World Spirit (*Weltgeist*), as in the case of the *Science of Logic*, which – like every science – is to point the way to truth, but – in contrast to formal logic – not only as a way to formal truth, but also to the real one.[39] The path of real truth must lead through ,and it does, not only logical principles such as the principle of the excluded middle, or the principle of contradiction, but also such ontological categories as the category of "being," "nothingness," "becoming," "existence" (*das Dasein*), "infinity" or "finiteness."

To these categories Hegel refers in the first parts of this dissertation, trying to show that logic is and should be treated as the logic of being, or – to use the modern term – ontics or the study of the particular forms of "beingness

---

[38] Cf. G. W. F. Hegel, *Phenomenology of Spirit*, op. cit., p. 416.

[39] To be more precise, Hegel divides logic into, primarily, subjective and objective logic, and secondly, into "logic of being" (*Logik des Seins*), "logic of essence" (*Logik des Wesens*), and "logic of the Notion" (*Logik des Begriffs*). Cf. G. W. F. Hegel, *Science of logic*, London 1969, p. 64.

of a being" (Seienheit). In the first book of this work, after having presented
"the general division of logic into the logic of being, the logic of essence and
the logic of the notion." he poses a question on "definiteness" ("pure being – without any further definitions" which turns out to be void, but not the
same as "pure nothing"), which, when expanded, turns out to be the matter
of the becoming of being in the process of the dialectical uniting of "being"
(beingness) and "nothingness" until such a moment is reached in which "Being
and Nothing are one and the same" ("This unity now remains their base from
which they no longer surface in the abstract meaning of being and nothing").

This enables a smooth transfer to the discussion of existence ("Existence is
a defined being"), its separation into "existence as such," finiteness and infinity,
and to showing both the ontic and logical side of these instances of beingness.
For example, the ontics of finiteness is a matter of the "boundaries of something", while its logic is either a negative or an affirmative definiteness of these
boundaries, and it must be emphasized that according to Hegel, this ontics and
logic "pass on to each other and into each other" until the "difference between
them vanishes" and complete Oneness is achieved. The case is similar with
infinity, which remains in a dialectical relation with finitude, and which reveals
its successive forms of beingness and logic.[40] Hegel devoted a substantial part
of the first book of the *Science of Logic* to the description and explanation of
the relationship between finitude and infinity. In its final sections, it appears
that these considerations are a kind of introduction to logic treated as the science of the essence, i.e. about "the absolutely undifferentiated oneness" ("This
oneness, assumed as a totality of determination in what way it is determined
in it as an undifferentiated oneness, is a many-sided contradiction").

The second book of the *Science of Logic* is dedicated to the "Doctrine of
Essence". Among others, Hegel answers the questions: What is this essence
(it is the "truth of being"), what is a pure being (it is "the sum total of all realities"), and how does this being emerge? (it emerges thanks to "the infinite
movement of being"), what is it at the beginning and at the end? ("Initially it is
a simple negation," or a being "for that which is different" and at the end "it is
a complex positivity" or "something in itself and for itself") and how this movement takes place "towards itself"? (This motion occurs dialectically). The last
of these answers, however, requires a number of additional, important details.

Obviously, such an addition can be found in his large volume of *The Science
of Logic*. Individual chapters of its first section titled "Essence as reflection

---

[40] "The infinite is: (a) in its *simple determination* affirmative as a negation of the finite; (b)
but this is in *alternating determination* with the *finite*, and is the abstract, *one-sided* infinite; (c) the
self-sublation of this infinite and of the finite, as a *single* process – this is the *true* or *genuine*
infinite." Cf. ibidem, p. 137.

within itself" are devoted to a succession of issues of "the appearance" (and within its framework to the "assuming" "external" and "defining" reflection), "The essentialities or the determinations of reflection" (such categories appear within them as "identity," "difference" and "contradiction"), and "Ground" ("absolute," "specific" and "real"). Section Two of this volume is titled "Appearance." The starting point for the reflections contained in it is the statement that "the being has to manifest itself". In the third section Hegel deals with reality ("reality is a unity of beings and existences"), and from these considerations is derived, among other things, a conclusion on the existence of three kinds of "totality of the reflective of proceeding" and on their ontological identity: "These three totalities are [...] one and the same reflection that, as *negative-self-reference*, differentiates itself into the other two totalities – but as into a *perfectly transparent difference*, namely, into the *determinate simplicity*, or into the *simple determinateness* which is their one same identity. – This is the *concept*, the realm of *subjectivity* or of *freedom*."[41]

The Hegelian logic of subjectivity deals with this realm of subjectivity and it is also called by this philosopher "a subjective logic," or to be more precise, "a system of subjective logic" since Hegel, also in this respect, wanted to be a thinker of systems and not one of the old style, but in a new fashion, i.e. one for whom such "a completely ready-made and solidified, one may say, ossified material is already to hand, and the problem is to render this material fluid and to re–kindle the spontaneity of the Notion in such dead matter." First, he answers the question: how is subjective logic different from objective logic – in the light of this answer, Objective logic "treats of being and essence constitutes properly the genetic exposition of the Notion," while the former deals with the "I, or pure self-knowledge," being – unlike the other – a functional "*exposition of the Notion*," i.e. in the applications of "*I*" in common understanding, in imagination, in memory, in sensations, in viewing etc. Further on, Hegel explains what these and still other functions of "*I*" are; for instance: understanding is "the power of creating Notions in general" ("But it is with reason that it is especially contrasted; in that case, however, it does not signify the faculty of the notion in general, but of determinate notions"). The problems of traditional logic – such as the issues of various judgments or various types of reasoning – also appear in these considerations, but they appear to be only specific concepts ("For the judgment and the syllogism or reason are, as formal, only a product of the understanding since they stand under the form of the abstract determinateness of the Notion").[42]

---

[41] Cf. ibidem, p. 571. The highlights were done by Hegel.

[42] "The I is the pure Notion itself which, as Notion, has come into existence. When, therefore, reference is made to the fundamental determinations which constitute the nature of

In the section titled "Objectivity," Hegel attempted to build a bridge (transition) between the objective logic and the subjective logic. First of all, he questioned the rationality of the solution proposed by Descartes (it is connected with the so-called ontological argument for the existence of God), using Kant's arguments in this critique, and then performed a critique of mechanism (which he saw as "an immediacy whose moments, by virtue of the totality of all the moments, exist in a self-subsistent indifference as objects outside one another"). He opposed mechanism to "chemism" ("The chemical object is distinguished from the mechanical by the fact that the latter is a totality indifferent to determinateness, whereas in the case of the chemical object the determinateness, and consequently the relation to other and the kind and manner of this relation, belong to its nature").[43]

The considerations closing this fundamental work are concerned, among other things, with the problems of the *purposiveness* ("Where there is the perception of a *purposiveness*, an *intelligence* is assumed as its author...") and the status of: ideas (it appears that ideas have both an ontological and epistemological status, which means that they are really "existing being[s] and objective truth[s]"), life "in itself and for itself ("life, considered now more closely in its idea, is in and for itself absolute *universality*; of objectivity which life has in itself"), and life as "the idea of cognition" ("*Thought, spirit, self-consciousness,* are determinations of the idea inasmuch as the latter has itself as the subject matter, and its *existence*, that is the determinateness of its being, is its own difference from itself...").

The final chapter of *The Science of Logic* is about the idea of the Absolute – as something that "emerges before us," and combines everything – the beginning and the end, becoming and having become, theory and practicality, objectivity and subjectivity, the object and subject, the real and formal, the general and particular etc. According to Hegel, "[the idea of the Absolute] is the sole subject matter and content of philosophy, Since it contains *all* determinateness within it, and its essence consists in returning through its self-determination and particularization back to itself, it has various shapes, then the business of philosophy is to recognize them. Nature and spirit are in general different modes of exhibiting *its existence*, art and religion its differ-

---

the I, we may presuppose that the reference is to something familiar, that is, a commonplace of our ordinary thinking. But the I is, first, this pure self-related unity, and it is so not immediately but only as making abstraction from all determinateness and content and withdrawing into the freedom of unrestricted equality with itself." Cf. ibidem, p. 583.

[43] In the summary to the section on Chemism, Hegel writes about the "transition of Chemism" between the world of the subjective and the objective, the formal and the real, the subjective and the objective, etc.

ent modes of apprehending itself and giving itself appropriate existence."[44] Its logical recognition (in the Hegelian sense of the word) has already been performed. Therefore, what remains for a philosopher is to make an attempt to recognize it in other forms and areas of manifestation.

Hegel made such an attempt, the results of which he presented first in a synthetic form in the *Encyclopedia of Philosophical Sciences* published in 1816. The word "encyclopedia" used in the title of this work means as much as that it is a draft presentation of all the relevant forms of the manifestation of the Absolute, or – which is just the same – an outline of Hegel's philosophical system; that system is of course a holistic expression of the Absolute.[45] The system consists of three parts, namely: the science of logic, the philosophy of nature, and the philosophy of spirit. And the *Encyclopedia* is divided accordingly. Its first part (which is the largest one) includes a repetition of the most important theses and postulates contained in the *Science of Logic*. In the end, Hegel formulates a general conclusion on the dialectical transition of such a being, that is, an idea into such another being which is natural; it "*resolves to release* freely *from itself* the moment of its particularity or the first determining and otherness, *the immediate idea*, as its *reflection*, itself as *nature*." The second part of the work, titled "The philosophy of Nature," is dedicated to this idea as a "reflection." In it Hegel repeats his objections to finite mechanics, and opposes to it absolute mechanics – as a science of "the matter in the freedom of its concept and which exists as being in itself"; Hegel closes the "Philosophy of Nature" with the statement: "In this way nature has passed over into its truth, into the subjectivity of the concept, whose objectivity is itself the suspended immediacy of individuality, the concrete generality, the concept which has the concept as its existence – into the spirit."

Of course, the final part of the *Encyclopedia* deals with the philosophy of this spirit. In the introduction to these considerations, Hegel writes that

---

[44] Cf. ibidem, p. 824.

[45] The circumstances of the writing of such an outline are explained by Hegel in the preface to the first edition of the work: "The need to provide my listeners with a guide to my philosophical lectures (at the time, Hegel was a lecturer at the gymnasium of Nuremberg – A/N) first prompted me to let this overview of the entire scope of the philosophy come to light earlier than I would have otherwise thought appropriate. The nature of an outline not only excludes a more exhaustive elaboration of the ideas in terms of their content, but also restricts in particular the elaboration of their systematic derivation, a derivation that must contain what is otherwise understood as a proof and that is indispensable for a scientific philosophy." Cf. G. W. F. Hegel, *Encyclopedia of the Philosophical Sciences in Basic Outline*, Cambridge 2010, p. 5. His second remark is significant, as it reflects Hegel's conviction that, when discussing reason, reasonableness, rationalism and rationality, it is necessary to have a significant amount of evidence for the formulated theses.

"the knowledge of Mind is the highest and hardest, just because it is the most 'concrete' of sciences," and he concludes that in the various sections is presented both the subjective and objective forms of the manifestation (extensive discussion of this issue is, of course, to be found in his *Phenomenology of Spirit*) in order to – according to the Hegelian logic – return at the end to absolute spirit ("it is an *identity* eternally existing in itself, as well as the one that returns to itself and which has returned to itself").

In the paragraphs ending the considerations contained in Hegel's *Encyclopedia*, the author points out the need to trace the manifestation of the absolute spirit in religion, art and philosophy. In religion this absolute spirit appears, among others, in the form of faith and cult, while in art in the form of beauty, while in philosophy, in the form of a concept. "This concept of philosophy is the self-thinking idea, truth aware of itself, or logic with the significance that it is generality preserved in concrete content. In this way science returns to its beginning, with logic as the result;" and further – when explaining departing of the absolute spirit from itself and returning to itself – he ascertains that this is based on: the first syllogism, "which has logic basically as its starting point, with nature for the middle term and is linked ultimately to spirit. Logic becomes nature, and nature becomes spirit;" whilst in the second syllogism: "the syllogism of reflection on the idea; his is a syllogism which is already the standpoint of the spirit itself [which] presupposes nature and joins it with logic;" and the third syllogism is "the idea of philosophy, which has self-knowing reason, the absolutely general."[46]

In his lectures written down some years later for students of the University of Berlin (in 1818 Hegel became head of the chair of philosophy of that university), there appears a number of important additions about this self-knowing, self-reflecting, and "delighted with itself" reason. In the *The Elements of the Philosophy of Right* published during Hegel's lifetime (1821), he formulated a statement frequently repeated in the future, "What is rational is real, what is real is rational." This statement is immediately followed with arguments which show that this rationality is not something given once and for all, but is in the process of becoming, consolidating itself and passing on in order to emerge from within itself – through its own "mechanisms" (laws of logic) – a new rationality (reality). The task of the philosopher and of philosophy is,

---

[46] "[...] a middle which divides itself into spirit and nature, with the former as its presupposition, and the latter as its general extreme. Thus immediate nature is only a posited entity, as spirit is in itself not a presupposition, but rather totality returning into itself. In this way the middle term, the self-knowing concept, has as its reality primarily conceptual moments and exists in its determinacy as general knowledge, persisting immediately by itself." Cf. G. W. H. Hegel, *Philosophy of the mind*, New York 2008, p. 197 ff.

of course, the *inquest into the rational*. "Hence it cannot be the exposition of a world beyond, which is merely a castle in the air, having no existence except in the terror of a one-sided and empty formalism of thought."[47]

After this programmatic declaration on rationality, or – what is just the same – rational philosophy, Hegel passed on to present that which is reasonable (at least to a certain point in time) in its "external existence." In the case of philosophy of law this is primarily the very idea of law – the idea of law itself, which is a reasonable "element" of law. Then he presented the distinction of law into: positive right (which "has validity in a state", among others, "through the particular character of a nation, the stage of its historical development, and the interconnection of all the relations which are necessitated by nature"), and abstract rights (it is also the law in force in some country, but "it is a free will not only in itself but for itself also"). What unites these two rights is freedom: "Thus freedom constitutes the substance and essential character of the will, and the system of right is the kingdom of actualised freedom. It is the world of spirit, which is produced out of itself, and is a second nature."[48] These two types of rights differ in their attitude to reality – in the case of the first one, it is a positive attitude in the sense that the will which constitutes "the substance and definition of law" is directed *towards external realities* (such as a family or state), while in the second case it is "the will, which, from the external existence, is a self-reflection." This means that will "exists in its *dissociation*," which manifests itself, among other things, in "civil society."[49] The latter becomes a state when it reaches the level of "the ethical spirit as substantial will, *manifest* and clear to itself, which thinks and knows itself and implements what it knows in so far as it knows it."

In the conclusions summarizing the *Elements of the Philosophy of Right*, Hegel states that the subject of universal history is not the states, nations or individuals, but the spirit of the world, to whom the former serve and for which "they are all the time the unconscious tools and organs of the world mind at work within them" – such as is the achievement of self-knowledge, self-realization and self-delight. Individual states and nations designate the steps towards this goal. In the final parts of this work Hegel lists four such

---

[47] Cf. G. W. H. Hegel, *Philosophy of Right*, New York 2008, p. xviii.

[48] Cf. ibidem, p. xxix.

[49] "Civil society contains three moments: (A) The mediation of need and one man's satisfaction through his labour and the satisfaction of the needs of all others — the System of Needs. (B) The actuality of the universal principle of freedom therein contained — the protection of property through the Administration of Justice. (C) Provision against contingencies still lurking in systems (A) and (B), and care for particular interest, as a common interest, by means of the Police and the Corporation." Cf. ibidem, p. 101.

"realms," which – like the recognition signals on the path to self-realization of the spirit of the world – show the distance it had covered. The last of these is the "Germanic Realm" – in it this spirit "grasps the infinite positivity of this its inward character, i.e. it grasps the principle of the unity of the divine nature and the human, the reconciliation of objective truth and freedom as the truth and freedom appearing within self-consciousness and subjectivity." In the *Lectures on the Philosophy of History*, which was written later still, in this specific apology of the "Germanic Realm," Hegel went even further, because he tried to prove – first, the superiority of the Protestant German countries over Catholic ones, second, the superiority of those who had adopted Lutheranism over all others, and third, the elevation, in the eighteenth century, to the highest level of rationality of the Prussian state and its ruler Frederick the Great.[50]

Looking holistically at the standards of rationality adopted and implemented by Hegel, one can say that they are all based on the assumption that the Reason in its historical march realizes itself both through affirmations and negations, while the relationship between them is of a dialectical character. This means that every affirmation encounters its negation, and every negation has its affirmation, and at the end of this chain emerges the main character of all the events, i.e. the "World Spirit" (*Weltgeist*). Preparing a complete list of Hegelian affirmations and Hegelian negations, however, would be a difficult task and perhaps even impossible to accomplish. Almost every page of his dissertations contains some affirmations and some negations, and the key to their proper understanding can sometimes be found at the beginning and sometimes at the end of these works. Anyway, in each case it turns out that the Hegelian Owl of Wisdom flies out at dusk, i.e. when the last of the major cards in this great battle for the rationality of philosophical thought and action has been revealed. This is, of course, only a metaphor, and – like any other metaphor – requires explanation and more details. In practice, it means the necessity of moving from the general into much detail, and from detail to many general statements; let us add – it is a transition according to the rules of the Hegelian logic, which – aspiring to the maximum of clarity – would also want to be the logic of such ambiguities in which everybody, who at least partly understands the nature and structure of the dialectical relationship, must encounter the nature and structure of the dialectical relationship. Adherence to this logic – understood as the logic in specific applications, as well as the

---

[50] "Frederick II demonstrated the independent vigor of his power by resisting that of almost all Europe," and his "merits [were] especial notive as [he] comprehended the general object of the State, and [was] the first sovereign who kept the general interest of the State steadily in view." Cf. G. W. H. Hegel, *The Philosophy of History*, Ontario 2001, pp. 457-461.

logic of being and beingness – requires a specific "road map" and, of course, the abilities to read this "map" properly.

All of these tasks are to be performed by Hegel's *Science of Logic*, hence the complex structure of its arguments. Simply following the logical order of affirmations and negations occurring in it requires quite extensive focus and philosophical experience. Admittedly, at the very beginning of the treatise there is an affirmation stating that "the matter and the content of these sciences is held to be independent of logic," but it turns out that in this sense, logic "can provide only the formal conditions of genuine cognition and cannot in its own self contain any real truth, not even be the pathway to real truth." Further on, there is an affirmation of Hegelian intellectualism, expressed both in the attitude to sensualism and common sense rationalism, and Kantian transcendental idealism. According to Hegel, each of these options had and has its own standards of rationality; however, these standards have been to some extent burdened with non-rationality and limited. He demonstrates this using rich and varied means, including philosophical metaphors used by his predecessors. As they are supposedly at a higher level of rationality, it unfortunately means the necessity of constructing still higher levels of abstraction, but also entering greater complexities of affirmation and negation. Such a "laboratory" example of these complications can be the Hegelian metaphor of the "Lord and bondsman." A rational answer to the question why "the Lord" (although he is "self-existent") cannot exist (as "Lord") without his "bondsman," and why the "bondsman" (even though he "wants to be free from his chains") cannot exist without his "Lord" is possible. What is unacceptable here, or is not acceptable rationally, is a simplistic answer, such as, for example, "It cannot, because it cannot." According to Hegel, what is real is rational, and therefore has its reasons. Thus the task of the rationalist philosopher and rational philosophy is to precisely locate and evaluate those reasons.

Postscript

An interesting contribution to the discussion on the rationality standards adopted and implemented by Descartes, Kant and Hegel may be the opposition of those philosophers to various entanglements of human thought and their attempts to free it from those entanglements. Obviously, their oppositions are different. In each case, however, its overall aim is an attempt at a complete rationalization of thought and action. What these philosophers have in common is also the conviction that this goal is potentially achievable and realistic, and their philosophy is its best evidence. Certainly, they differ in the perception of the path leading to it, and the views on how to follow it, as well as in their intellectual means and ways; but none of them has any doubts about the fact that here one must refer to the intellect.

In Descartes' *Meditations* what is exhibited most strongly is the opposition against sensualism (confidence in the reliability of the senses, presented by the philosopher as the road leading astray) and scepticism (doubt for doubt's sake, seen by him as a cognitively destructive behaviour). However, in his *Discourse on the Method* this opposition is more diverse and varied, because both the cognitive value of various sciences as well as common beliefs are questioned. Nevertheless, neither the former nor the latter is considered to be totally useless in this realization of a great undertaking, which is achieving an absolutely certain and absolutely true knowledge. However, in both discourses relatively little attention is paid to the problems that preyed on the most original and daring minds of the Renaissance, i.e. the rationality of divine creationism, the rationality of the sciences, which referred to this creationism, and the rationality of those who use them in their thinking and action, and which they teach in schools. Indeed in the *Discourse on the Method* these teachings and these scholars are mentioned, but the reader can conclude that either they do not represent any rationality, or they represent such a rationality that is not worthy of that reader's exertions. However, although the Great Maker is mentioned twice in the *Meditations*, he first appears as a potential Great Cheater, and later – when it turns out that he is not a cheater – a philosopher, using his intellect, which assigns him the function of someone who is supposed to ultimately shut the gate through which falsehood might get into his thinking.

From the point of view of Kantian rationality standards, Cartesian oppositions, although reasonable, are not sufficient to avoid internal contradictions, paralogisms and antinomies, namely, the things that do not allow human thought to becoming rational or cause it to cease being rational. However, the direction taken by Descartes in the search for certainty and truth is generally considered by Kant to be accurate; he also finds Descartes' attempts to rid that path of the ballast of sensualism or that of scepticism to be partly successful, or at least be justified. The main problem which his predecessor could not ultimately overcome was criticism and self-criticism, more precisely, lack of its application where it should be used. Not using it caused a gate to be left open for the facade of consistency, facade of rationality, etc. The way out from the world of appearances, proposed by Kant, is among other things, to make a clear distinction between the world of pure reason and the world of practical reason. In the former there is place for the Cartesian meditating "I," but there is no space for his recourse to God, the guarantor of the reliability of this meditation. Although there is no place for such a God as understood by Descartes, in this world of God it is expected not to give cognitive, but moral guarantees, and these two issues should not be mixed, because it is irrational in itself and must lead to different irrationalities. The price, which Kant was willing to pay for this "kingdom of Pure Reason" (and "pure rationality") was an agreement to waive the intellectual efforts of crossing the border between the world of thought (phenomena) taken at large and the world of things in themselves (noumena). Descartes – like many of his predecessors in philosophy – was not prepared for it either mentally or intellectually. In this, among other things, the fundamental difference between the two great philosophers lies.

Hegel was not so much insufficiently prepared mentally and intellectually to come to terms with the inability of crossing that border, he was rather convinced that its marking had neither logical nor ontic grounds (reasons). However, a central problem in his philosophy is not an attempt to identify where this "superstition" comes from, but an attempt to show and prove that all the boundaries between that which is spiritual and that which is corporeal are and should be crossed, and that the main task of human reason and human rationality is to recognize how and why they are crossed. But it is not human reason that plays the main role in this philosophy, rather it is the Omni-mind, called the Spirit of the World. If for the former there is something difficult to reconcile with, it is precisely with the fact that in the end it turns out to not be the Lord that reigns over the whole world. The human mind is not just any servant, because its task is to bring historical events to such a happy ending which is the return of the true Lord to himself, and of himself to that house about the erection of which first and then the inhabiting of it second so many pre-Hegelian philosophers dreamed and talked. However, along this path, an obstacle was present in either the subjective or objective point of view. According to Hegel, the art of rational thinking consists in the ability to dialectically combine both points of view. This implied the entanglement of the human mind not only in the philosophical but also historical, social, religious, and many other issues. This entanglement of reason in these different spheres of reality, however, cannot be resolved by anything other than by reason itself. At one point it appears to be common sense, other times as something as uncommon as intellect; one time it is individual reason, sometimes it is a collective mind; once it is practical reason, while at other times it is pure reason, and still another time it is a pure practical reason, etc. Recognizing when and why any of these roles occur is also the task of reason. Hence, its consciousness and self-consciousness appear to set the next steps leading to this Oneness which, like a Platonic light at the end of the road, attracts the attention of the rationalist philosopher and allows him to keep to the proper direction of thinking and acting.

Therefore, it can be said that philosophical reason is *the heart* of Hegel's philosophy. If, however, human life was primarily or exclusively about rational philosophizing, the matter would be relatively simple; but it is not its only meaning – of which, after all, this philosopher was well aware. Therefore, we must add that there is no real rationality without perceiving the multidimensionality of human life, and attempts at reducing it to one or only several dimensions can indeed have some reasons behind them, but they never are and never will be sufficient reasons. This remark particularly applies to such philosophers as Descartes and to Cartesian philosophy as such; still even in the centuries that followed, there was no shortage of such reductionists.

Chapter IV

Philosophy of science of the twentieth century

1. Henri Poincaré

Already during his lifetime, Henri Poincaré (1854-1912) had become a well-known and recognized scientific authority (not only in France) – especially in such sciences as mathematics and theoretical physics.[1] Like other prominent intellectuals of the time, he commented not on only scientific but also philosophical issues. His name used to be associated with the so-called conventionalism, understood as a particular kind of philosophy of science.[2] Studying his works convinces the reader that although he was self-taught in the field of philosophy (he received a university education in mathematics and technology, first at the École Polytechnique and later at the École National Superieure des Mines), he could see in the exact sciences not only their principles or laws, but also their general rules, including the principles of their development in the past and in the future. He presented these in his dissertations: *Science and*

---

[1] This recognition was expressed, among other things, in the number of honorary doctorates he was granted. The list of these honours is provided by D. Leszczyński and K. Szlachcic in: *Wprowadzenie do francuskiej filozofii nauki*, Wroclaw 2003. The authors emphasise that "his contemporaries and researchers of later generations described him as a genius and placed him along with such authorities as Isaac Newton, Carl F. Gauss or Albert Einstein." Ibidem, p. 66.

[2] In the light of this philosophy, "certain theorems of exact sciences, mistakenly thought to be descriptions of the world based on registers and generalizations of experience, are actually artificially produced works, and the motive of their recognition is not the coercion of empiricism, but other considerations, above all comfort, intellectual profit, and also aesthetic values." Cf. L. Kołakowski, *Filozofia pozytywistyczna. Od Hume'a do Koła Wiedeńskiego*, Warsaw 1966, p. 145.

Hypothesis (1902), *The Value of Science* (1905), and *Science and Method* (1908). They were written in the form of essays, with the liberty characteristic of this genre, and with digressions and references to persons and problems which at that time were at the centre of attention of philosophers and scientists. This way of writing on important issues in France has had a long tradition (dating back to the time of M. Montaigne). Poincaré characteristically combines intellectually sophisticated theses and hypotheses with all sorts of allusions and figures of rhetoric; often it is difficult to distinguish where the theses end and the rhetoric begins.

The *Value of Science* was one of his works written in such a narrative. It can be compared to Descartes's *Meditations on First Philosophy*. Although the name of the latter philosopher is not mentioned even once, the initial problem of these philosophers-scientists is the same, and is expressed in the question in the title of *Meditation I*, "What can one doubt?" Poincaré supplements it with an additional question: "What do those who pose the question of the value of science doubt?"[3] Generally, however, in both cases the premise is the same, that is, it deals with reasons (in the strictest possible sense) for such doubting, which will not be destructive but cognitively constructive, or, freeing human thinking from errors, and leading to truth. Already in the first sentence of this dissertation its author states that "the search for truth should be the goal of our activity; it is the sole worthy goal of them."[4] The answer to the question about the roads leading to achieving this goal is put by Poincaré in a broader context of criticism of four types of cognitive extremes. He put them into mutually complementary and mutually exclusive pairs. The first of these pairs is extreme intellectualism and extreme scepticism, while the second is extreme logicism, which he called analytism, and radical empiricism.

Although he rarely mentions the names of the representatives of these extremes in science and philosophy, at least in some cases one can guess whom he means. And so, in his criticism of extreme intellectualism, he surely means Descartes, among others. The evidence that this is so is not only the repetition of the question used in the title of *Meditation I*, but also his reference to the

---

[3] Among those "others" is first of all Édouard Le Roy, author of *Dogma and Criticism*, a work published at the time of the writing of *The Value of Science*. More about this philosopher and his views, who is poorly known in Poland (and often erroneously represented), can be found in the work already quoted here, i.e. *Wprowadzenie do francuskiej filozofii nauki*. The authors of this book accurately observe that Le Roy was believed by his contemporaries to be firstly "a radical Catholic modernist" (i.e., a religious thinker), and only secondly as a philosopher of science (radical conventionalist). Today, the latter opinion seems prevalent (when referring to him in discussions on the value of science).

[4] Cf. H. Poincaré, *The Value of Science*, in: idem, *The Foundations of Science*, New York 1913, p. 205.

Cartesian philosophical comparison of constructing a philosophical system to the erection of a building (a house); in *The Value of Science,* he refers to "the rebuilding of a city, where the old buildings are demolished to make room for the new ones." Poincaré agrees with the author of *Meditations on First Philosophy* as to the need to approach everything critically, but he is against transforming this criticism, "into ruthless demolition of time-worn buildings" to the very foundation. He compares such action with the work of Penelope, who raises "ephemeral structures," which are "soon forced to [be] demolish[ed] from top to bottom" by their builders "own hands." The consequence of such conduct, in science is treating scientific theories as something impermanent, accidental, and not really worth remembering – in the light of the standpoint of extreme intellectuals: "today the theories are born, tomorrow they are the fashion, the day after to-morrow they are classic, the fourth day they are superannuated, and the fifth they are forgotten" and it only depends on the will of those intellectuals whether they will last a day longer or shorter. Of course, this is arbitrary, and thus irrational (it is not backed up by strong reasons).

Poincaré similarly accuses sceptics of arbitrariness and irrationality. Characteristic of their standpoint are to be the "desperate convictions" that, first, "it is not possible to save any of the values of sciences," and, second, that human language cannot adequately express the mental states experienced by man. Consequently, this – as it is defined by the authors of the *Value of Science* – "anti-intellectualist philosophy," "condemns itself to being intransmissable" (incapable of transferring information – A/N), or – which means the same thing – is "a philosophy essentially internal, or, the very least, only its negations can be transmitted." An example of such philosophy is, for him, the views of Édouard Le Roy; in the light of these views the "intellect deforms all it touches, and that is still more true of its necessary instrument 'discourse,'"[5] Therefore, the only thing that is left for the sceptics is the "act of desperate faith" in some kind of superhuman strength, which will save them from this infirmity, i.e. the recourse to divine help. It is worth recalling that still the extreme intellectualism represented in such views (in its Cartesian version) also was forced to seek God's support. Although Poincaré does write about this in *The Value of Science,* his criticism of such extremes, aims, among other things, to prove that they converge in their final consequences.

It is also evident in his criticism of the approach of the analysts. He accuses them of a tendency to put everything into final and irrefutable formulas. This procedure is compared by him to the procedures of the French builder

---

[5] Cf. ibidem, p. 323. Also, he adds (recognizing his opponents general intentions spot-on) that if LeRoy "regards the intellect as incurably powerless, it is only to give more scope to other sources of knowledge, to the heart, for instance, to sentiment, to instinct or to faith."

of fortresses, Vauban, "who pushes on his trenches against the place besieged, leaving nothing to chance." This is to give them a sense of complete assurance and a conviction about the absolute accuracy of the cognitive results obtained. Poincaré does not claim that their cognitive procedures are not certain, or that the results they obtain are not true. He says, however, that they do not enrich our knowledge semantically; about the search for the land desired by them, which is "a completely pure logic," i.e. a logic which is not implicated either in psychology or physiology, he wrote that it "could never leads us to anything but tautologies."[6] In the *Value of Science* he accuses them of using "an artificial language" and solving problems that are so simple that they do not require any specific evidence. An example of an analyst who multiplied the number of problems was for him the mathematician Méray who considered it doubtful that "an angle may always be subdivided" and "to prove it he needs several pages."

In *The Science and Method* the list of those analysts who vested too much hope in logic is much longer, and the accusations are more numerous. Among others he writes about a school of those who are "abounding in ardor and full of faith" and which attempts to reduce mathematics to logic.[7] One of the members of such a school is the mathematician George F. L. Cantor whose attempt at reductionism led to the so-called Cantorian antinomies, or contradictions.[8] To this school also belongs David Hilbert, who attempted to prove the logical consistency of geometry – to this end he "reduced to a minimum the number of the fundamental assumptions of geometry and completely enumerated them." Poincaré does not accuse him of contradictions as such. However, he accuses him that he is not capable of closing this list of axioms because "in reasonings where our mind remains active, in those where intuition still plays a part, in living reasonings, so to speak, it is difficult not to introduce an assumption or a postulate which passes unperceived" in the reasoning.[9] He also accuses him of a more or less conscious mechanism, i.e. an attempt to reduce "all the geometric reasonings to a form of purely mechanical [ones]" and of the art of geometry to the art of a chess player shifting figures on the chessboard. These and other limitations and shortcomings of the art of analysis prompted scientists to search for a new logic. The most interesting effort in this field was considered by Poincaré to be the logic of B. Russell – the "logic

---

   [6] Cf. ibidem, p. 215. A little further, he adds: "it could create nothing new; not from it alone can any science issue."

   [7] Cf. H. Poincaré, *Science and Method*, in: *The Foundations of Science*, New York 1913, p. 448.

   [8] "These contradictions have not discouraged them and they have tried to modify their rules so as to make those disappear which had already shown themselves, without being sure, for all that, that new ones would not manifest themselves." Cf. ibidem, p. 449.

   [9] Cf. ibidem, p. 451.

of propositions," which proposed "the study of the laws of combination of the conjunctions *if, and, or*, and the negation *not.*"[10] Its advantage is that it is much richer "than the classic logic; the symbols are multiplied and allow of varied combinations which are no longer limited in number." However, its weakness or imperfection was, among other things, the impossibility of "proving the principle of complete induction without any appeal to intuition." In his conclusions to the criticism of Russell's standpoint and that of other analytical logisticians, he states that this replacing of some statements by other ones ("which we may be tempted to regard as a new truth") so characteristic of them, will lead to that "there will finally remain only identities, so that all will reduce to an immense tautology."[11]

At first glance, such an approach is supposed to be fundamentally distinct from the approach of the empiricists. For them anything that depends only on the mind is not evident "by itself," and neither is it evident as a result of formal and logical operations. However, what is supposed to be obvious are the so called experimental facts, also called at the time "pure" or "raw;" that is, the ones that are not entangled in any theory, any assumption, any language and so on.[12] In *Science and Hypothesis*, Poincaré calls this approach to facts by the name of "naive dogmatism" and he makes an attempt to prove its groundlessness, indicating among other things its followers dependence on the language in which those facts are expressed and presented; "and our language is made up only of preconceived ideas and can not be otherwise. Only these are unconscious preconceived ideas, a thousand times more dangerous – than the others." Thus he asks: "If we introduce others, of which we are fully conscious, we shall only aggravate the evil" And he responds "I think not. I believe rather that they will serve as counterbalances to each other – I was going to say as antidotes."[13]

In *The Value of Science* he enriches this argumentation with reasons indicating an analogy between the "purely logical" facts of the analysts and the "purely experimental" facts of the empiricists. However, in *The Science and Method* he

---

[10] "And this is, I think, a most happy idea, because the classic syllogism is easy to carry back to the hypothetical syllogism, while the inverse transformation is not without difficulty." Cf. ibidem, p. 460.

[11] Cf. ibidem, p. 485. He adds: "He does not add a new wing to the building, he saps its foundation."

[12] How varied was the understanding of fact in the French philosophy of that time is shown by Barbara Skarga in her dissertation *Kłopoty intelektu. Między Comte'em a Bergsonem*, Warsaw 1975, p. 14.

[13] "[...] they will in general accord ill with one another – they will come into conflict with one another, and thereby force us to regard things under different aspects. This is enough to emancipate us. He is no longer a slave who can choose his master." Cf. H. Poincaré, *Science and Hypothesis*, in: *The Foundations of Science*, New York 1913, p. 129.

points to another clue against "naive dogmatism" which leads to real rationalism; it is constituted by the fact that "we can not know all facts, since their number is practically infinite. It is necessary to choose; then we may let this choice depend on the pure caprice of our curiosity; would it not be better to let ourselves be guided by utility, by our practical and above all by our moral needs; have we nothing better to do than to count the number of ladybugs on our planet?"[14]

It is also worth making a note of the presence in *The Value of Science* of a criticism of utilitarianism. It expresses Poincaré's opposition, first against the excessive exposition of practical criteria in the evaluation of science (assessing them from the point of view of their social usefulness), and second, to the reducing of the basic sciences (such as astronomy and theoretical physics) to social problems. He accuses these attempts not so much of naivety as short-sightedness and falling into internal contradiction.[15] In *Science and Method* he submits his *vote of separation* from the matter of usefulness in favour of which most of his contemporaries are, i.e. the usefulness combined with "industrial applications, miracles of electricity or motoring." He also has objections against such a usefulness that boils down to "making man to be a better man."

Before answering the question in favour of whose utility he is inclined, he says that "the scientist does not study nature because it is useful; he studies because he delights in it, and he delights in it because it is beautiful. If nature were not beautiful, it would not be worth knowing, and if nature were not worth knowing, life would not be worth living. Of course I do not here speak of that beauty which strikes the senses, the beauty of qualities and of appearances [...] I mean that profounder beauty which comes from the harmonious order of the parts and which a pure intelligence can grasp." This "intellectual beauty is sufficient unto itself, and it is for its sake, [...] that the scientist devotes himself to long and difficult labors."[16]

---

[14] Cf. H. Poincaré, *Science and Method*, op. cit., p. 362. By no means is the answer to this question an easy one. On the one hand, this calculation can be treated as a manifestation of naive belief that in the end it will be possible for us to count all these "ladybugs"; on the other hand, it may be an encouragement to look for such solutions which might make this undertaking more efficient – Poincaré considers as such making choices of the most interesting facts, and these appear to be "facts which can be used several times; those as to which there are the most chances that they will recur. [...] Thus, which facts have a chance to recur? First of all, these are simple facts. [...] But do simple facts exist, and if yes, how to identify them?"

[15] "Auguste Comte has said somewhere that it would be idle to seek to know the composition of the sun, since this knowledge would be of no use to sociology. How could he be so short-sighted? Have we not just seen that it is by astronomy that [...] humanity has passed from the theological to the positive state? He found an explanation for that because it had happened." Cf. ibidem, p. 294.

[16] Cf. ibidem, p. 367.

Each of the above options is considered by Poincaré to bring scientists closer to the truth to some degree, but none of them takes it to such a degree as the one he proposed and which can be called – in contrast to Descartes' philosophical intellectualism – a scientistic intellectualism. In the postulative part of *The Value of Science* he presents his assumptions, theses and postulates. They are addressed to the relatively small group of people who consider the search for truth as "the only worthy goal of life" and – which is not less important – who wish and are capable of devoting their lives to attain this objective.

Indeed in *The Value of Science* there is no comprehensive description of these people; however, from his remarks that appear in different places in his work, a certain idea of a scientist emerges. This scientist is such a person who sets before him maximalist goals, while realizing at the same time that these cannot be attained quickly or in a foreseeable future. It is also someone who lives in suffering and discontent ("absence of suffering is a negative ideal, which could most likely be gained by the annihilation of the world"). He does not mean any dissatisfaction or any suffering, but such that make the scientist not cease to pursue the truth (even though "the truth is often cruel," and sometimes he is "scared by the truth").

To the question of how this image, or the idea of a scientist, refers to the standards of rationality adopted by Poincaré, there are no unequivocal answers. However, one can guess at least so much that in them there are not only the logical arguments that are meant in them, but also in the non-logical sense of the word, i.e. those "reasons" which a logician – in the old or a newer style – will be willing to put within inverted commas; and he will act in such a way for both the psychological and historical "reasons" in science. He will act similarly in relation to the reasons considered by Poincaré as the essence of the life of a scientist, e.g., such as the ones that were pointed out by him in the final paragraphs of *The Value of Science*; here he writes, among other things: "We must suffer, we must work, we must pay for our place at the game, but this for seeing's sake; or at the very least that others may one day see." For logicians (analysts) these kinds of statements do not and cannot represent cognitive value.[17] They are too ambiguous and do not really lend themselves to logical control. However, in Poincaré's opinion they either express deep wisdom (rationality) or they almost "touch" upon it. A logician has the right, and perhaps even an obligation to ask: "Do they touch or do not touch, and what does it mean that they touch?" This is because according to him, the

---

[17] He adds, in a similar fashion: "All that is not thought is pure nothingness; since we can think only thoughts and all the words we use to speak of things can express only thoughts, to say there is something other than thought, is therefore an affirmation which can have no meaning." Cf. ibidem, p. 355.

gate leading to truth must be closed. According to the author of *The Value of Science*, of course, it would be well if it was closed down, but not at the cost of closing the road to something new and at the same time cognitively significant. In other words, this or that in logical accuracy needs to be sacrificed for the sake of psychological depth.

For this thesis, which is difficult to accept (not only for logicians, but also for mathematicians), he gives in *The Value of Science* extensive explanations and thorough justification, which consists of elements of both the scientific knowledge and the life wisdom of a scientist. Here at least three mutually complementary blocks of arguments can be distinguished. In the first of them Poincaré points to the subject sources of scientific knowledge and describes and explains their function, in the second similar and analogical cognitive operation in relation to object sources, while in the third one he defines the status of science (recognized as a result of the activities of scientists). The totality of these arguments is supplemented with an attempt to answer the question about the status of the material (natural) world. The appearance in this dissertation of these blocks of arguments and of this question is another argument in favour of the already formulated thesis that the author fits within the formula of post-Cartesian thinking or - in other words – is a Cartesian scientist of a new type.[18] Moreover, this dissertation can be regarded in some sense as a repetition of Descartes's *Meditations on First Philosophy* – a repetition which contains critical components, which, in turn, make important corrections to the Cartesian standpoint.[19] Therefore, it is worth taking a somewhat closer look at these arguments.

It begins with an indication of the subjective sources of knowledge. They appear to be the senses, the imagination and the mind. The general question posed by Poincaré, however, concerns not so much what these sources are, but rather what the rules of their functioning are, and what their cognitive fertility is. When answering these questions, he argues that:

---

[18] I consider as a post-Cartesian each philosopher and scholar, who – like Descartes – first, "turns from the naive to radical objectivism" and turns in the direction of "transcendental subjectivism", second, adopts "the idea of universal science", third, assumes that such science is "a possible goal of possible practice", and fourth that this universal science must have the form of a deductive system. E. Husserl, after whom I quote these characteristics of a post-Cartesian scholar, adds: "the all-embracing science must have the form of a deductive system, in which the whole structure rests, *ordine geometrico*, on an axiomatic foundation that grounds the deduction absolutely." (cf. E. Husserl, *Cartesian Meditations*, The Hague 1982, p. 7). Thus, I shall add that I distinguish a post-Cartesian from "a Cartesian philosopher" by just this that for the former a hypothetical-deductive foundation will suffice, while the other feels sure only on the axiomatic-deductive foundations.

[19] For more on this subject, cf. Z. Drozdowicz, *Les Meditations cartesiennes d'Henri Poincare*, in: *L'esprit cartésien, Actes du XXVe Congres de l'Association de Philosophie de Langue Francaise*, edites par: B. Bourgeois et J. Hevet, Paris 2000, p. 1097 (et plus loin).

1. The senses are a kind of adaptability to the stimuli of the external world by the human physiological structure, and that this structure represents a functional whole, that is, "a group of sensory fibers," in which action and reaction are synchronized with each other; in this synchronisation the following rule applies: "the minimum of one's own forces – the maximum of benefit;" "this principle is an expression of unconscious opportunism" (this is the first of the clues that lead to understanding of the mysteries of the above-mentioned "gate") that which is an effect of sensory activity is a "nebula of impressions;"

2. Imagination is the ability to break down this "nebula" to elements, i.e. "surfaces as the boundaries of solids or pieces of space, lines as the boundaries of surfaces, points as the boundaries of lines." The appearance of these three and only three elements is a confirmation that the imagination is guided by the principle of the "minimum", which "bears" not only elements ordering the "nebula of impressions," but also various contradictions;

3. The basic function of the mind is reduced to the elimination of these contradictions, an elimination in such a way that having to choose a number of different options (such as e.g., "one can choose between a space of four dimensions and three-dimensional space"). As a rule he selects those that either contain a minimum of contradictions or minimize the chance of their appearance; another important and complementary function of the mind first comes down to "a slight push" ("*un coup de pouce*") of the imagination and senses to work more closely together, which allows to prevent contradictions (this is the second of the clues leading to the knowledge of the mysteries of this "gate"); the mind does it due to the same "unconscious opportunism" as it did previously.

In the second of the Poincaréan blocks of arguments in question, he analyzed such objective sources of knowledge as concepts, theorems and scientific theories, i.e. as they are called by the author of *The Value of Science* "delicate constructions that are entirely mind-made." The thing, however, concerns only those "delicate constructions," which appear in mathematics, astronomy and physics. Poincaré is not interested in the other sciences at all, or his view is that they are dependent on the mind to a too small degree to be considered as capable of generating "subtle intellectual constructions."

Therefore, mathematics:

– provides scientists with "a convenient way of speaking" ("our ordinary language is too poor, it is besides too vague", to express the relations that are "so delicate, so rich and so precise" with which we deal in science);

– gives them into their "hands" rich means of reasoning, especially reasoning by analogy (allowing "to rise above the chaos of observation" and to see "hidden harmony");

– is helpful to scientists in developing "the sense of symmetry" and "the sense of simplicity."

The dependence between mathematics and astronomy, and physics is, according to Poincaré, mutual. To justify this thesis he gives several examples of such mathematical problems which have their origins in physics such as an integer or discontinuous functions. In turn astronomy:

– shows the scientists "how small is man's body, how great his mind" ("since intelligence can embrace the whole of this dazzling immensity, where his body is only an obscure point, and enjoy its silent harmony");

– encourages scientists to trust the mind and distrust the senses;

– improves their imagination; thanks to astronomy "imagination, like an eagle's eye that the sun does not dazzle, can look truth in the face," including such general truths as the one that a. everything in the Universe is subject to the same dependencies; b. these relationships constitute such a harmonious whole that the mind of a scientist can "enter into a relationship with it;" c. this "entry into a relationship" gives him a chance to approach "infinitely precise laws;" d. those laws are essentially simple, and their simplicity should "serve him as a good teaching," etc.

Poincaré's analysis of such a subjective source of knowledge as physics is more complex. Poincaré puts it in two complementary historical perspectives, i.e. its past and future history. In the first he distinguishes two stages of the development and progress of this science – the lower one, called by him "the physics of central forces" – and the higher one called "the physics of the principles". A comparison of each of these stages leads him to formulate a general conclusion that "we are on the eve of a major change" in physics and that these changes will be "beneficial" to it; "maybe we will have to build entirely new mechanics, which would be, above all, characterised by this fact, that no velocity could surpass that of light."[20] This part of the text is full of such general conclusions. These include, among other things, statements that: 1. in physics, there has been a constant progress; 2. it owes this progress mainly to astronomy (before it became an independent field of studies it "imitated astronomy," e.g. by "treating atoms like astronomy treats stars"); 3 the appearance of the idea of "central forces" was the result of a too faithful following of astronomy, till, however, the "day arrived when the conception of central forces no longer appeared sufficient" and physicists replaced it with "certain general principles." Explaining and justifying the last of these generalizations he indicated that: 1. the principles of physics were "the results of experiments boldly generalized" ("to a large extent their generalizations"); 2. "they seem to derive from their very generality;" 3. still, they are not absolutely certain, this

---

[20] Cf. ibidem, p. 312. It is worth noting that these theses were formulated during the time when Albert Einstein formulated his specific theory of relativity. His article on the matter was published in "Annalen der Physik" in September of 1905.

being highlighted by the contradictions that appear in them and between them; 4. these contradictions "impose on our common sense with irresistible force." This does not mean that they have no cognitive value. However, it does mean that – like the "concept of central forces" – they have a historical value (a relative one), relativized to the level of the mental development of scientists.[21]

All these generalizations concern that what was and what currently is in physics. In *The Value of Science* there are also some predictions about what is going to appear in the future, and what will appear, among others, are simpler, easier and more reliable theories and, of course, those scientists who will be able to properly evaluate and appreciate this simplicity, convenience and certainty. Each of the blocks of arguments distinguished ends with scientists, sometimes mentioned by name, but mostly as a group characterized in different ways, who want and know how to use reason (to think and act rationally).

The Poincaréan conception of conventionalism in science fits this characteristic. The occurrence of the conception is directly connected by Poincaré with such an activity of scientists as their shift in scientific procedures from "raw" facts to scientific facts, and then from scientific facts (which are a collection of individual "things") to the scientific laws (which are a collection of "universals," which he called "scientific decrees"). At each stage of this procedure there is an elimination from the facts of that which is random and uncertain, and extraction from them of that which is in its own way necessary and defined. These facts gain value through the rational activity of scientists such as the use of cognitive procedures tested in science, the use of the laws and principles already existing in science or the coming to conclusions by scientists through various kinds of agreements.

In relation to scientific facts, questions can and should be asked whether they are or are not true, but 'if you put the question to me: Is such a fact true? I shall begin by asking you, if there is an occasion, to state precisely the conventions, by asking you in other words, what language you have spoken; then once settled on this point, I shall interrogate my senses and shall answer yes or no."[22] This question is unreasonable in relation to the principles of science, since "principles and conventions" are adopted by scientists, not because of their truthfulness, but because of convenience or ease. Convenience has nothing to

---

[21] Such as: (Meyer's) law of the conservation of energy, (Carnot's) law of the degradation of energy, (Newton's) law of action and reaction, the law of relativity (in its light, the "laws of physical phenomena are to be the same for the unmoving observer as well as a moving observer moving with a regular translatory motion"), the principle of the preservation of mass (of Lavoisier), or the principle of "minimum effort – maximum effects" (Poincaré ascribed its authorship to himself).

[22] Cf. H. Poincaré, *The Value of Science*, op. cit., p. 328.

do with arbitrariness (randomness) or irrationality. But it has a lot in common with the necessity and rationality. In *The Science and Hypothesis*, Poincaré admits that principles are only the decrees and edicts which are "the product of free activities of scientists." Soon, however, he adds that these decrees are not arbitrary, but are conditioned by membership in the world in which we live, and "if transported into another world (that I call the non-Euclidean world and seek to imagine), then we should have been led to adopt others."[23] In *The Value of Science* he points to the reasons that make that these decrees can be and are rational.

To put it in a nutshell, these reasons are connected: 1. with such specific mental abilities as different types of intuition (Poincaré distinguishes logical, mathematical and sensual intuition); 2. with such basic cognitive criteria as simplicity (regarded by him as a criterion of truthfulness) and convenience (considered as the criterion of certainty); 3. auxiliary criteria such as: beauty (of theories, theorems, etc.), provability by experience, or the frequency of the successful completion of the action taken. None of these reasons is either an axiom itself or gives absolute certainty to the results achieved in science. However, some of them more, others less, bring scientists and science closer to certainty. For example, logical intuition (also called by him "a pure one") gives the greatest certainty, but at the same time has the relatively narrowest field of view, while the sensuous intuition, based on the imagination, has the relatively widest field of view, but gives relatively least certainty.

These criteria appear to be here not (as is the case with Descartes, for example) signs of such fundamental cognitive values as certainty and truth, but the determinants of the choice of different, yet in each case relative, cognitive values (scientific concepts, theorems and theories, etc.). This means that using the first of these criteria – of two or more concepts, theorems, or theories one should choose those that are simpler; while using the second one, of two or more concepts, theorems or theories one should choose the ones that are more convenient.[24] In *The Value of Science*, these attributes are hierarchized – what is more important is convenience, and simplicity is less important. This means that if we consider something to be simpler, it is because it is more conveni-

---

[23] "Our decrees are therefore like those of a prince, absolute but wise, who consults his council of state." Cf. H. Poincaré, *Science and Hypothesis*, op. cit., p. 28. This "council of state" is, of course, a group of scholars competent in a given field or discipline.

[24] Poincaré illustrates it via the example of "the simultaneity of two events" – in the conclusion to this example, he says: "Thus, we take these rules (of measuring time – A/N) not because they are true, but because they are the most convenient, and we may recapitulate them as follows: The simultaneity of two events, or the order of their succession, the equality of two durations, are to be so defined that the enunciation of the natural laws may be as simple as possible. In other words, all these rules, all these definitions are only the fruit of an unconscious opportunism." Cf. H. Poincaré, *The Value of Science*, op. cit., p. 234.

ent, but not the other way around. This hierarchization (and hierarchization in general) is one of the principles of Poincaréan rationalism.

To sum up, for this rationality, a standard is such a conduct which, although it does not lead a scientist to obtain the absolute certainty and truth of scientific facts (theories, laws and principles), will still lead him to those the reliability and accuracy of which will be relatively the greatest of the ones that are possible (at a given moment of the development of knowledge). To achieve this, a scientist will not only carefully and repeatedly analyze that which is the subject of his research, but will also cooperate in this field of studies with other scientists, and confront his results with the results obtained by them, and – as far as possible and appropriate – confront them with empirical data (the results of experiments). However, he will not yield to "the coercion of empiricism," because there are few people as aware as he is that confronting scientific facts ("these complex and subtle concepts") with raw facts leads, or at least should lead, to the fundamental differences between them. It is obviously the scientist who is aware of his uniqueness and even superiority over all those who yield to "the charms" of a more or less naive objectivity. However, he can justify and indicate the error of those who yield to these "charms". He wants and knows how to work effectively with a group of other scientists who are, although not numerous, relatively the most efficient and intellectually capable – while maintaining the distinctiveness of their sciences and their methods of cognition – of bringing something of value to science. To the question of how they should behave in relation to this group of representatives of other sciences, and other philosophical options than that which emerges from Poincaré's considerations, we actually do not find in his essays any clear answer, but one can guess that he expects from them either adaptation (including the adaptation of the standard of rationality adopted by him), or he condemns them to wander astray within the pseudo- or quasi-sciences. It should be emphasized that the door he left open for speculation or risky hypotheses regarding the question of the determinants of the conduct of genuine scholars in genuine science is only for genuine scholars, and Poincare does not include in this group psychologists or sociologists and not even those philosophers who do not base their philosophy on mathematics, astronomy or physics.

2. Neopositivistic standards

Between the standards of rationality adopted by the ideological founder of positivism, Auguste Comte (1798-1857), and the standards of the followers of this philosophy of science in the twentieth century, there are such profound differences that the latter used to be called neopositivists or logical positivists. In their standards remains, however, what Comte himself called "the spirit of positive philosophy" and which he presented in the *Discourse on the Positive Sprit*, a work described as "the systematic manifesto" and compared to Descartes' *Discourse on Method*.[25] Answering the question: what should be combined with that spirit, he briefly stated that it must be combined "with impartial moderation" and the "voluntary and selfless zeal, supported by common sense and the ever more favourable general situation."[26] These general or even vague and imprecise statements were concretized and made precise in his above mentioned dissertation. In the light of the considerations contained therein, it appears that this is a systematicity and systemicity, although similar to the one that the great systematists of modern times tried to realize, but in the opinion of Comte more rational than the other because it exceeds its limits and weaknesses and leads to a higher synthesis of everything that was positive (rational) in the past. An expression of this synthesis is to be, among other things, combining the historical point of view (called by him *dynamic*), with the suprahstorical or extrahistorical one (called by him *static* or *dogmatic*), then that which is the general with that which is specific, that which is sensual with that which is mental, that which is collective with that which is individual, etc. The list could go on, as "the spirit of positive philosophy" has aspirations of being a spirit of new universalism.

A component of this universalism is the Comtean understanding and systematisation of the sciences. It combines the dogmatic point of view with the historical one; "the former consists in arranging sciences sequentially according to their dependency in such a way that each is based on the previous one and prepares the next; the latter systematisation recommends such an arrangement of sciences which corresponds to their actual emergence so that one comes from the former to the latter."[27] Both points of view are "after all" to relate to "humanity as the only completely universal concept", but they refer to it in different ways, since in the first of them Mankind is expressed ontogenetically, while in the other it is expressed phylogenetically. However, they have led to the same conclusion, namely, to the distinction (and to justification of this distinction) of the six basic academic disciplines, i.e., mathematics, astronomy, physics, chemistry, biology and sociology. As part of this systematisation (called by Comte an *encyclopedia of sciences*) is the division into sciences preparing for "significant scientific research" and those sciences conducting these studies – and

---

[25] Cf. *Letter to J. S. Mill* (of June 19, 1842), in: A. Comte, *Correspondance inedite*, vol. 1, Paris 1903.

[26] Cf. A. Comte, *A General View of Positivism*, London 1908, p. 355.

[27] Cf. ibidem, p. 360.

this differentiation is relative. This means that science, which from one point of view may be regarded as preparing the studies, from another point of view can even be regarded as conducting "important research." In this way, sciences can be divided into those that are "an introduction to the study of the external world" (Comte included mathematics and astronomy within them), and those that explore this world (he included physics, chemistry and biology within them). In turn, these latter disciplines are to be "an indispensable introduction" to the study of the social world and the "indispensable basis" for sociology, a discipline which investigates social phenomena and "reveals their rather complex conditions". It should be added here that in the Comtean positivism, the possibility of reducing higher sciences to lower ones is negated both as far as the methodological reduction (reducing to the same research methods) is concerned as well as the ontological one (reducing to the study of the same kind of dependencies, regularities, laws or principles). Comte was decisively against such attempts at reduction undertaken by his contemporary "physicists-chemists", on the one hand, and by "mathematicians-astronomers", on the other.[28]

Comte's main intention to compile this *encyclopedia of sciences* is clear. The point is to transfer this furthest-reaching rationality, which is characteristic of mathematics – only step by step – onto the sciences which investigate more complex relationships and dependencies than maths does. Among others, this is confirmed by those Comtean characteristics of the notion of *positive*, in the light of which means "the ability to create spontaneous harmony of logic in the mind" and "logical accuracy." In practice, this is to mean rational thinking, with signs of its basis being clarity and logical coherence. But it should also be noted that in the light of the *Dissertations on the Positive Spirit*, in "the paramount sense" *positivity* means that which is "organizing" and "contributing" something really new to all that to which Mankind has ever been striving; and it was striving and still strives to the ever greater rationality not only of its thinking, but also of its practical activities and its social life.

The representatives of logical positivism were reluctant to endorse such a broad program of rationality and rationalization. They co-founded the so-called Vienna Circle, i.e., a group of philosophers, logicians and mathematicians who met regularly at the University of Vienna and discussed the problems of the philosophy of science, in particular, the possibility of liberating it from speculativism and investing it with a fully scientific character.[29]

---

[28] In his opinion, "the empirical tendency" occurring in the former ones leads, among other things, to an "incessant instability of concepts," while "the pride of being at the real source of positive rationality," among other things, leads to "halting [the] human mind at the very initial stage of solid theoretical development." Ibidem, p. 370 ff.

[29] The Vienna Circle was established in 1926 by Moritz Schlick, and among its members were Gustaw Bergmann, Rudolf Carnap, Herbert Feigl, Philipp Frank, Kurt Gödel, Otto Neurath,

Such an attempt at dealing with speculativism in philosophy is Hans Reichenbach's (1891-1953) work titled *The Rise of Scientific Philosophy*. In this work he begins with a critique of the speculativism of ancient philosophers, including those who were considered in some measure as the greatest authorities in the field of philosophy. The list of accusations against them is long and varied. Generally, one can say that these philosophers did not observe such elementary requirements as science is supposed to meet, such as language, the formulation of meaningful sentences, or such generalizations that result "from the material collected during observation." "A classic illustration of this type of fallacy can be found in the philosophy of Aristotle (384-322 BCE) when he treats of form and matter. Geometric objects present the aspect of a form as distinct from the matter of which they are built; the form can change while the matter remains the same. This simple daily experience has become the source of chapter of philosophy which is as obscure as it is influential and which is made possible only by misuse of an analogy."[30] Reichenbach is equally critical of the philosophy of Plato, as in his opinion, "it is based on one of the strangest and yet one of the most influential philosophical doctrines – the theory of ideas" and – like the philosophy of his disciple, Aristotle – is an expression of the abuse of analogy ("Plato considered exploring the ideas as a source of knowledge similar to the observation of real objects, but much higher than the former as revealing to us the necessary properties of objects"). In conclusion to this critique of the ancient philosophical authorities, Reichenbach states that "science ends once the thirst for knowledge is satisfied by pseudo explanations, by confusing analogy with generalisation and by the use of metaphors in the place of well-defined concepts."[31]

This critique is an introduction to an attempt at answering the question about the rationality of knowledge. Although in Plato's philosophy there are some valuable indications in this respect, e.g., the negation of the value of such sensual cognition and exposing of the value of mathematical knowledge ("Plato regarded mathematics as the supreme form of all knowledge"), still, "the modern scientist, despite his use of mathematics as a powerful instrument of research, would not accept this maxim unconditionally" since the "empiri-

---

Hans Reichenbach and Friedrich Waismann. To find more on this topic, cf. H. Buczyńska-Garewicz, *Koło Wiedeńskie. Początek neopozytywizmu*, Warsaw 1960; L. Kołakowski, *Filozofia pozytywistyczna...*, op. cit., Warsaw 1966.

[30] "The form of the future statue, Aristotle argues, must be in the block of wood before it is carved, otherwise it would not be there later [...]. It is obvious that this inference can only be made by the help of vague usage of words. [...] I have used Aristotle's doctrine of form and matter as an illustration of what I have called a pseudo explanation." Cf. H. Reichenbach, *The rise of scientific philosophy*, Berkeley 1951, p. 12.

[31] Cf. ibidem, p. 14.

cal science in the modern sense of the word is a successful combination of mathematical observational methods. Its results are regarded, not as absolutely certain, but as highly probable and sufficiently reliable for all practical purposes. To Plato, however, the concept of empirical knowledge would have appeared an absurdity."[32] This philosopher, however, was a rationalist in his own way, because "this word and its adjective *rationalistic*," "refers to a philosophical method that considers reason as a source of synthetic knowledge about the world and does not require observation to verify the knowledge." In the same way the rationalists were such philosophers of the modern era as Descartes (who "claimed to have proved the existence of the ego by logical reasoning; I think, therefore, I am, so goes his magical formula") or Kant ("who claims to have found synthetic *a priori* in the principles of mathematics and mathematical physics"). According to Reichenbach, Kant's philosophy, indeed, "surpasses the philosophy of his predecessors, Plato and Descartes, in this that it avoids the mistakes committed by them;" however, it is not rational either ("the term *rationalistic* must be precisely distinguished from the term *rational*"), because "the ground on which he built was not as firm as he believed it to be," and this ground was the recognition of Newton's physics as the supreme achievement of knowledge and its idealization into a philosophical system.[33]

It is worth noting that the standpoint taken by Poincaré is considered by Reichenbach to be only "an extension of the theory of Kant." However, a completely different position in the history of rationalism is awarded to Socrates ("who considered virtue as a form of knowledge" and "presented the ethical viewing as an equivalent of geometric viewing"), Spinoza ("who in his ethics imitates an axiomatic construction of geometry given by Euclides, believing that it will help him to embed ethics on the grounds just as sure as the grounds of geometry") and Hegel ("the starting point of Hegel's philosophy is not science but history," while the point of its arrival is "the primitive simplification, worthy of a novice, who constructs his own philosophical system"). As a certain continuation, but also a modification of Hegel's rationalist system, Reichenbach recognizes the dialectical materialism of Karl Marx ("yet in his fundamentals, Marx is the greatest opponent of Hegel because he refuses to share Hegel's primitive belief in the power of reason"). In conclusion to the presentation and criticism of these philosophical standpoints, he states that

---

[32] "The idea of mathematization of knowledge, of physics which is of the same type as geometry and arithmetic, springs from the desire to find absolute certainty for the laws of nature." Cf. ibidem, p. 31.

[33] "In deriving from pure reason the principles of Newtonian physics, he believed he had achieved the complete rationalization of knowledge, had attained the goal which his predecessors had been unable to reach." Cf. ibidem, p. 43.

between the rationalistic philosophy and rational science there is a chasm. "The rationalist philosopher is anti-scientific from the very roots of his mind. The path of his thoughts is determined by extralogical motives which employ scientific results and methods as instruments for the attainment of non-scientific aims." Reichenbach sees no future for such a philosopher. He sees it, on the other hand, for such philosophers and such philosophy that is "related to science and [has] already responded to many questions posed by philosophers in earlier periods of time."

Before answering the question of which philosopher and philosophy he means here, he performed a critical analysis of empiricism, a philosophical option treated since ancient times as the opposition to rationalism. "Philosophers of this type regarded empirical science, and not mathematics, as the ideal form of knowledge; they insisted that sense observation is the primary source and the ultimate judge of knowledge, and that it is self-deception to believe the human mind to have a direct access to any kind of truth."[34] In ancient times these philosophers were Democritus, the creator of the atomic theory and his follower Epicure, and Sceptics such as Karneades ("who laid the foundations of empiricism in the intellectual circles") and Sextus Empiricus ("who was one of the representatives of the empirical school of physicians"). The list of these empiricists-philosophers is much longer in modernity; the "great empirical systems" of F. Bacon, J. Locke and D. Hume appeared at that time, the systems in which "the theses of empiricism could witness lucid formulation". These theses boil down to an exposition of the role of the senses and minimize the role of the human mind ("empiricism reduces the mind to a subordinate role"). Reichenbach presents both the positives and negatives of this option, along with its the development during the period – it is supposed to be expressed in the gradual departure from "Bacon's naive inductive logic" and arriving at a conviction that the truly scientific logic of induction "cannot be fit within the framework of Newtonian physics," and support in the "20th century physics should be looked for."

In the further part of his dealing with the speculative past of the philosophers and philosophy, Reichenbach presents the relationships of empiricism and rationalism with classical physics. In the light of these arguments, the Greeks' contribution was significant "almost exclusively in the mathematical sciences," and in empirical science only insofar as "they used the methods of mathematics." An important breakthrough in this regard has been made only in modern times and is associated with the names of such scientists as Copernicus and Galileo.[35] After them came the next generations of empiricist scientists,

---

[34] Cf. ibidem, p. 75.

[35] "With the establishment of the heliocentric system, Copernicus laid the foundation of modern astronomy and, at the same time, gave the decisive turn to modern scientific thought,

who "addressed questions to nature and left it to nature to answer yes or no."
A person intellectually towering over other scientists was the founder of classical physics, Isaac Newton. Reichenbach presents him not only as a brilliant
physicist (a discoverer of several laws of physics), but also as an excellent
methodologist (an inventor of the "new mathematical method, namely the
differential calculus"), an experimenter and philosopher ("courageous enough
to take the risk of interpreting that which is abstract" and "at the same time
cautious enough not to believe it until it was confirmed by the facts").

Parallel to modern empiricism and its applications in physics, modern
rationalism was developed; it remained not only in opposition to empiricism,
but was also the philosophy which made attempts at applying its solutions in
physics and other natural sciences. Of intellectual caliber, comparable to that
of Newton, were both Leibniz ("who developed the theory of space based on
the relativity of motion, in which he anticipated the logical rules of Einstein's
theory of relativity") and Kant (who tried to show that "the foundations of
physics are the product of reason"). The final balance is such that the "rationalistic interpretation of classical physics could not solve these problems,
which were put forward by the empirical interpretation." This situation was
the starting point for those philosophies of science that emerged in the nineteenth and twentieth centuries, including the philosophy which Reichenbach
calls a *scientific* one.

In the next few parts of his dissertation, Reichenbach makes several
references to these philosophies. He is less interested in the solutions they
proposed, and more in the problems they undertook, as well as both the errors
they made and the successes they achieved. "In the light of these arguments,
the greatest successes were achieved by those philosophies of science, which
as far as possible could benefit from the 'wealth of technical inventions' and
"'wealth of logical analysis.'" On the other hand, the defeats were suffered
not only by those sciences which did not know how to use them, but also
those sciences and those scientists who could not understand that they would
not properly solve the problems undertaken until "they find answers to some
more general questions, questions of philosophical character. Their luck was
that they could look for these philosophical answers, without being hampered
by some philosophical system. Thus, for each problem they could find an
independent answer [...]. In this way, guided by the logic of the problem, they
found answers of which the philosophers did not dream." The thing is not
even in the fact that in the nineteenth century no system was born (because
such systems can easily be found on the pages of philosophy textbooks), but

---

emancipating it from the anthropomorphisms of earlier periods. Galileo gave to modern science
the qualitative experimental method." Cf. ibidem p. 98.

in the fact that they were like a kind of "drying up river," and also in the fact that philosophers of a new type appeared – "the men who made it were hardly philosophers in the professional sense. They were mathematicians, physicists, biologists or psychologists," and "their philosophy resulted from the attempts to find solutions to problems encountered in scientific research."[36]

Reichenbach attempts to establish which of the sciences generated actual rational problems and solutions, and how they did it, and, step by step, pushed back the speculative philosophy. He included within these sciences geometry (both Euclidean and non-Euclidean). Also, he engages in a polemic with H. Poincaré's standpont, "according to whom geometry is a matter of convention and a sentence the aim of which is to describe geometry of the physical world is nonsensical." In his opinion, we can reasonably speak of a "geometry of the physical world" or "natural geometry," but "provided that we shall determine in advance the coordinative definition of congruence."[37] He treats the analysis of the development of geometry, "in the historical cross-section," as "a perfect illustration of the philosophical possibilities contained in the development of science" and as the basis to formulate a general conclusion that "the forces of reason should not be sought in the regulations imposed by the reason of our imagination, but in the ability to free ourselves from all kinds of regulations imposed on us by experience and tradition." He listed among those sciences also mathematics, presented as a discipline dealing with the nature and structure of time, among others, its uniformity, metric properties, concurrency, etc.[38] He also included within them contemporary astronomy, physics, biology and all those disciplines that examine, describe and explain the principles and laws of nature – such as the principle of causality, repeatability, regularity or the irreversible phenomena occurring in nature.

From the analysis of these teachings, he derives a number of metatheoretical and methodological conclusions. To the first of these can be included the distinction of the laws of statistics ("they are valid not only in games of chance," but also "in many other areas," including the social sciences), adopted by the scientists and in their principles realized by them in formulating theories (e.g. such as the principle of atomism, or the principle of determination). In

---

[36] Cf. ibidem, p. 123.

[37] "Poincare was right if he wanted to say that the choice of one from the class of equivalent descriptions is a matter of convention. But he was mistaken if he believed that the determination of natural geometry, in the sense defined, is a matter of convention." Ibidem, p. 134.

[38] In the conclusion of his considerations of time he states that "what we feel as the flow of time has been revealed to be identical with the causal process that constitutes this world. The structure of this causal flux has been discovered as being of a much more complicated nature that is exhibited by the time presented in direct observation..." Cf. ibidem, p. 155.

contrast within the second, methodological ones, he included the problem of interpretation and the interpreting of rules and laws ("it deprives the law as the accuracy and makes it only a probability"), observing and describing the phenomena, including the language of description ("truth is not limited to one language"), experimentation and the interpretation of the results of experiments, deductive and inductive reasoning, etc. Reichenbach concretizes these metatheoretical and methodological problems on the example of the evolutionary process discovered by Charles Darwin.[39] All this does not only have something of the spirit of Comte's positivism, but also something of the letter of his works. Without much trouble one can recognize here both Comtean metatheoretical and theoretical distinctions as well as its methodological injunctions. Starting from part fourteen of *The Origin of Scientific Philosophy* elements appear which essentially correct and supplement the classical positivism. These include the distinction of "predicative knowledge," i.e. such in which predicates are not semantically empty, they are not empty as to their content nor are they exclusively a development of the content found in the premises of reasoning. A logical foundation of such knowledge is the logic of induction. It is a logic which, although it does not achieve complete knowledge and truth, its contrasted, deductive logic, leads, and in any event can lead, to knowledge of a high degree of probability. It can lead to it provided that: 1. It will come from the observation of those facts which are "a fixed quantum of knowledge;" 2. It will not confuse the context of discovery (with the elements present in it like speculation or guessing) with the context of justification (with such of its elements as logical arguments, or logical analysis); 3. It will make the theory of probability a basis of making judgements about truth and falsehood; 4. It will reject the rationalistic interpretation of probability (lack of reason is considered by rationalists as a reason "authorizing to accept the equality of probabilities"), and the empirical philosophy of probability will be adopted.[40]

In the important additions to these general assumptions and methodological postulates there is an indication: a. to give priority to verification over falsification, b. to give priority to quantitative research over the qualitative one,

---

[39] "It was the great discovery of Charles Darwin that the apparent teleology of living organisms can be explained in a similar way by combination of chance and selection [...]. So we shall always depend on an inference from systematic order to historical order..." Cf. ibidem, p. 198.

[40] "The empiricist philosophy of probability is based on the frequency interpretation. Probability statements express relative frequencies of repeated events, that is, frequencies counted as a percentage of the total. They are derived from frequencies observed in the past and include the assumption that the same frequencies will hold approximately for the future. [...] It is true that for the frequency interpretation the degree of probability is a matter of experience and not of reason." Cf. ibidem, p. 236.

c. the need of reducing general statements to individual ones, and the latter to particular facts ("it is worth ascribing sense to sentences on the probability of particular facts if everyday experience provides us with a sufficient number of similar facts"). At the end of this list of assumptions and postulates it is indicated that this is "the key to understanding the predicative knowledge." It is the concept of "assumption" (*posit*), without which no knowledge can do. In the case of predicative knowledge, "we try to match our assumptions so that they should turn out to be true as often as it is possible. The degree of probability is a kind of *evaluation* of an assumption: it tells us how much good is our assumption. And this is the only function of the probability."[41]

In the section entitled *Functional Conception of Cognition*, Reichenbach opposes his conception to the transcendental conceptions characteristic of speculative philosophy (in their light, cognition "goes beyond observable objects and depends on sources other than the senses"), and he points to its general purpose (it is to be such a function as predicting the future). However, in the section entitled *The Nature of Ethics* he is against combining knowledge with normative ethics ("knowledge does not in fact contain any normative parts and thus it does not lead by itself to such an interpretation of ethics"). The analysis he carried out leads him to conclude that "moral directives are inherently volitional, i.e. they express volitional decisions of the person enouncing them." However, they are not arbitrary (this would lead to anarchism), but are "designated by more fundamental goals" than the wishes of individuals, i.e. the goals "determined by the environment of the group in which we live." Although both on these conditions as well as on these goals of scientific philosophy we cannot speak with such a high degree of probability as it is done by a mathematician or a physicist ("this results from the imperfection of today's sociology"), generally we can say that: 1. the "Ethical orientation of human society is the result of mutual adaptation"; 2. "the conflict of willingness is the driving force of moral development" and 3. "Power is that which supervises social relations." This does not have much in common both with knowledge as well as faith (e.g., in that "the struggle for power is controlled by a superhuman authority, that leads it to an absolutely good end"). These additional details also retain a lot of the spirit and letter of Comte's positivism.

Rudolf Carnap (1891-1970) modified this positivism in such a way that in the philosophy of systems it has become the analysis of the language of sci-

---

[41] "If we have a posit of the rating 5/6 and one of the rating 2/3, we shall prefer the first, because this posit will be true more often. We see that the posit does not tell us anything about the validity of a statement, but rather serves as a clue for choosing the assumptions." Cf. ibidem, p. 240.

ence. He also titled his programmatic dissertation in this manner. The starting point in it is the negation of the rationality of metaphysics, which is identified as speculative philosophy, or – which is just the same – with "those propositions which claim to represent knowledge about something which is over or beyond all experience, e.g. about the real Essence of things, about Things in themselves, the Absolute, and such like."[42] Within metaphysical claims he included the speculations of ancient philosophers (e.g. on the "matrix of all things") and the speculations of modern and contemporary philosophers (such as Spinoza, Hegel and Bergson). In short, these are metaphysical propositions which "have no empirical meaning," and statements about "the real world as a whole" do not possess any such meaning ("because the real existence of anything is nothing else but the possibility to locate this something in a certain system"). According to Carnap, a metaphysical character is also applicable to the general assumptions and statements of Comte's positivism and the "philosophy of moral values or moral norms, which can be called normative ethics."[43]

Responding to a question of what metaphysics is, Carnap states that it is one of the possible forms of expression ("metaphysical sentences – like lyrical poems – perform an expressive function, but do not perform an assertive one"), forms which open an extensive research field for empiricist psychologists ("psychological statements belong to the realm of empirical sciences like statements of chemistry, biology, historiography," etc.). However, he objected to such a merger of psychology with logic, which consists in "dealing with logical question as if it were a psychological one. This mistake – called Psychologism – leads to the opinion that logic is a science concerning thinking, that is, either concerning the actual operation of thinking or the rules according to which thinking should proceed."[44] In his view, logic is and in any case should be a logical analysis, i.e., an analysis of the logical syntax of language ("the logical syntax of a language is understood as a formal theory of this language"), i.e., the analysis of: 1. "the rules of construction of a language system;" 2. the transformation rules of some language system; 3. syntactic terms; 4. L-rules ("rules of transformation of a logical or mathematical character will be called the L-rules"), F-rules (physical rules), and L-terms and F-terms; 5. the content of a sentence ("the content of a given sentence is the set of consequences which are not binding statements"), in its theoretical and assertive sense, as well as material or formal mode.

---

[42] Cf. R. Carnap, *Philosophy and Logical Syntax*, London 1935, p. 15.

[43] "The propositions of normative ethics, whether they have the form of rules or the form of value statements, have no theoretical sense, are not scientific propositions (taking the word scientific to mean any assertive proposition.)" Cf. ibidem, p. 25.

[44] Cf. ibidem, p. 34.

The material mode "often leads to misunderstandings and futile philosophical disputes, which can be solved by translation of divergent theses into a formal mode." He performs a more comprehensive analysis and indicates that "if we wish to avoid the dangerous material mode, we must avoid the word 'thing' and instead use a parallel syntactic term 'thing-designation;' analogously, instead of the word 'number' we have to use the term 'numerical designation;' instead of the word 'quality' we should use the term 'quality-designation;' instead of 'relation,' 'relation-designation' [...]" etc. Using this method of translation of the material mode into the formal mode, we free the logical analysis from any references to non-linguistic subjects themselves and deal only with the shapes of the expressions of the language, etc.[45] Such translation is required, among other things, by such modal concepts as "possibility, impossibility, necessity and contingency," which turn out to be "actually masked syntactic sentences; these are sentences formulated in the material mode."

In conclusion to this analysis of language modes, he poses a question: "Can the same observations also refer to all other problems, including philosophy?" His answer is affirmative. However, he makes a reservation that the philosophy in "the meaning adopted here does not include [...] either metaphysics or psychology." But it includes "epistemology, or the theory of cognition," in which – "after the elimination of metaphysical and psychological components – remains the logical analysis of knowledge or, more precisely, the analysis of logical testing and verification of statements, as knowledge is the same as the whole of positively tested statements." In respect of such a domain of philosophy, which "enjoys interest today" and which is the philosophy of nature, it means a syntactic analysis of the rules by which material expressions are constructed or transformed (e.g. such as time and space) into a formal expression. In addition to this postulated reductionism, he points to the physical language as to the "language in which one can express all that is expressed through other scientific languages."[46] This language is to be the basis for the unity of science – certainly, the formal and not the material unity ("Physicalism and the thesis of the unity of science have nothing to do with such theses as monism, dualism or pluralism"). All these assumptions and postulates may be classified as the meta-theoretical part of his concept of knowledge.

Its elements are the theoretical issues of importance and verification. "The first one concerns the conditions of meaningfulness of sentences: in what conditions the sentence has a meaning – the meaning in the sense of cognitive

---

[45] Cf. ibidem, p. 70 ff.

[46] "In other words, every sentence of any branch of scientific language is equipollent to some sentence of the physical language, and can therefore be translated into the physical language without changing its content." Cf. ibidem, p. 89.

factual content. The second issue relates to a method of gaining knowledge: how can we determine that the sentence is true or whether, on the contrary, it is false. This second question implies the first. To determine whether the statement is true, we must of course understand this sentence, i.e. to know its meaning. But from the standpoint of empiricism these issues are in an even closer relationship. Actually, there is only one answer to both questions. If we know of what the verification of a sentence would consist, thereby we know what this sentence means."[47] According to Carnap, one should rather talk about the verifiability (confirmation) of a sentence rather than verification, because if the latter term "means the final, definitive establishing of truth" then no "(synthetic) sentences can be considered to be verified." This confirmation connects with the "process of growth of the degree of verifiability", and refers to those cognitive functions that lead to this verification – such as defining logical concepts ("belonging to the logical syntax"), bringing them (their reduction) to "the most important predicates" ("The most important kind of predicates that occur in the language of science, the predicates referring to the points of time-space"), or the formulation of "introductory chains" ("A finite chain of sets of sentences is called an introductory chain"). All these activities and their likes are recognized by him as "the logical analysis of confirmation and testing."

In contrast to this, "the empirical analysis of confirmation and validation" concerns "the empirical applications of language" i.e. to the determining of "what conditions must be satisfied by a sentence or a predicate of some language to have an empirical meaning." To this end, Carnap accepts – "as the starting terms" – the notion of an "observation" predicate and a "realized" predicate. In the case of the former a person can "in proper circumstances decide on the basis of little observation of the full sentence," that is it is "confirmed to such a high extent that it will either be recognized or rejected." While in the second case, this person "can in proper circumstances make this full sentence true, i.e. produce P property at the b' point."[48] In the light of this analysis, this decidability of the truth is – generally speaking – the degree of probability, and this finding is relativised to, first, the language spoken by the person, and second, it is relativised either to the observations this person makes or to the observation conditions created by this person. In any case, "if confirmation is to be a feasible task, this process of referring to the subsequent predicates must end somewhere. Ultimately, the reduction must lead to predicates, which can reasonably be confirmed directly, i.e. without reference to other predicates."

---

[47] Cf. ibidem, p. 94.

[48] "Whenever we use terms like 'observational', 'realized', 'verifiable' without reference to a person, these terms then should be understood as related to persons using language L, to which the discussed predicate belongs." Cf. ibidem, p. 141.

This puts in focus the problem which in classical positivism boils down to the statement: "every time the language of science is reducible to terms describing the sensory data." According to Carnap, this thesis requires a "major adjustment," because this positivism arbitrarily assumes a finite set of sentences, and that we operate the "language of things," i.e. such a "language, which we use to talk about perceptible physical objects that surround us in everyday life." Thus, he proposes to recognise first "the physical language" ("physical language contains in itself the language of things and also these terms of science which are needed for the scientific description of processes occurring in inanimate nature"), second, to recognise theses of "physicalistic confirmation," and third, to adopt "sufficient reduction bases," in which there are "sufficient definitional bases," "sufficient confirmational bases" and "sufficient testing bases." While in "physical language" it is possible to distinguish "several extremely narrow bases, which, however, constitute sufficient confirmational bases for the physical language and at the same time sufficient testing bases for the predicates of this language," still "neither the existence of such narrow bases nor circumstances that the just mentioned predicates are sufficient bases, is by no means a logically necessary fact. Reducibility is conditioned by the binding of certain universal sentences, thus by the system of adopted physical laws; the above mentioned facts are thus some peculiar features of the structure of this system or – to use the material mode – specific features of the causal structure of the world."[49]

In the further parts his work, Carnap analyses not "the structure of the world," but rather makes an analysis of: 1 the "construction of the language system," distinguishing in it "construction rules" (including types of sentences and types of operations of sentence construction), and "transformation rules" (including "L-rules" and "F-rules"); also the "Logical analysis of language," i.e. semantics and syntax distinguishing in it "pragmatics of language" ("the whole of studies in which the first component of language is taken into account will be called pragmatics"), "semantic systems," rules of different systems, their terms, logical syntaxes, and calculi. The two final parts of the dissertation are devoted to the calculus.

In the section entitled *Calculus and Interpretation* he asks the question: "is logic a matter of convention?" or – what in his opinion is reduced to the same thing – "or are the rules upon which the logical deduction is based to be the subject of free choice and therefore be evaluated only in terms of convenience, not correctness? Or, conversely, whether objectively correct or objectively incorrect rules can be distinguished, and while constructing the system of rules we have freedom of choice in relatively trivial matters (e.g. as to the way

---

[49] Ibidem, p. 157.

of formulating) meanwhile in all the important aspects we are constrained by certain limitations?"[50] In these questions are contained two essentially different problems, namely, that of the selection of rules of deduction ("syntactic transformation rules") and the matter of the choice of "the system of logic." Answering these questions, he states that "logic or deduction rules [...] can be determined by arbitrary choice, so they are conventional if they serve as a basis for the construction of the language system," while "the system of logic it is not the matter of free decision – if the interpretation of logical signs is determined beforehand. But even here conventions play the main role, because the foundation on which logic is built, namely the logical interpretation of the logical signs (e.g. through designation of truth conditions) may be the subject of free choice."

In the section entitled *Calculi and Their Application in Empirical Science*, he states first that "the main function of the logical calculus in its applications in science is not providing logical statements, i.e. the L-true sentences, but in directing deduction leading from factual premises to factual conclusions," and secondly, that "among factual sentences we will distinguish the *individual* and *universal* sentences."[51] Here he also gives examples of sentences of the first and second type, and formulates general remarks on both logical and extralogical calculus. Among other things, it is stated that "it would be virtually impossible to make any deduction, which is sometimes carried out, from a complete argument in a logical calculus, i.e., break it down into individual steps, each one would be an application of one of the rules of transformations of the calculus (with definitions)". Practically, it is possible to divide "a small fragment of this process" and then "to expand to the desired extent." An example of such a fragment is an elementary mathematical calculus ("usually interpreted in terms of numbers and numerical functions"), and an example of such an expansion are both wider mathematical calculi as well as those physical calculi which "assume as their position some logical-mathematical calculus, e.g. calculus of real numbers..." In the light of this reasoning, what "can be constructed in this way [is], e.g. the particle mechanics calculus" and "as a result of interpretation, the calculus theorems are transformed into physical laws, i.e. sentences that describe some characteristics of a universal event, they constitute the physical

---

[50] Cf. ibidem, p. 170.

[51] "By singular statements of scientific language, or an interpreted calculus, we shall understand statements about one or several physical objects (or actions, or points in time and space); for example, a statement saying that this or that object has this or that property, or that between those objects there is this or that relation. By universal statements we shall understand statements concerning all objects in a given field, for example, all physical objects, or all points in time and space". Ibidem, p. 200.

mechanics as a factual theory equipped with factual content, which is possible to test on the basis of results of observation."[52]

Generally, this is the same idea which appears in A. Comte's *The Encyclopaedia of Sciences* and which boils down to such a directing of deduction, while sticking to the most rigorous rules of formal logic, to transfer this degree of certainty and truth, which is a logical reasoning on to other sciences. Carnap restricts this transfer to empirical science, and particularly to the physical sciences. However, he also formulates a prognostic thesis that this development of physics, which in "the last centuries, and especially in recent times, led to the application on an increasing scale [...] of the method, which we call *formalisation* [...], will increasingly allow to dispense with 'intuitive understanding' of abstract terms and of axioms and theorems formulated by their means", and to replace them with "factual sentences" also in those disciplines which are currently based on "metaphysical sentences."

3. Karl Raimund Popper

Karl Raimund Popper (1902-1994) attempted to identify such standards of rationality that could be reduced neither to logic nor to mathematics, nor to any other scientific discipline which traditionally had shown relatively substantial rationality. Of course, he referred to these disciplines, but he also referred to the philosophical traditions that were the base for the version of rationalism that he proposed. However, he was critical of both groups. Moreover, from this criticism and self-criticism, which complemented the former, he made one of the trademarks of his standpoint. This criticism and self-criticism is used by him both in tackling and analyzing different issues. Of course, not always is it accompanied by attempts to define it so that the reader would not confuse it with those forms that had appeared previously in philosophy and with which Popper would not always agree on his way to achieving *objective knowledge*, i.e. that which, in his opinion, philosophers and scholars have sought for centuries and which they should still seek. That is why he titled one of his last works: *Objective Knowledge.*

In the Preface to its Polish edition Popper writes that "talking about objective knowledge, does not mean knowledge that is particularly certain, on the contrary – all our knowledge, especially scientific knowledge, is the knowledge that is full of conjecture, it is a hypothetical knowledge. Knowledge can be objective in the sense that we give it a form made of words and submit it to discussion in an impersonal way. In this discussion are considered the arguments

---

[52] Cf. ibidem, p. 230.

for it and against it. On the other hand, one should not discuss the motives that lead people to present these hypotheses."[53] In his other important work, *The Open Society and Its Enemies*, there is a fairly general, but also clear linking of rationality and rationalism with self-criticism, that is, "an attitude of admitting that I may be wrong and you may be right, and by an effort, we may get nearer to the truth."[54] This approach to rationality and rationalism is part of the critique of this "prophetic philosophy," for which the provider of facilities and ideological arguments is historicism. It is well worth taking a closer look at it.

In the aforementioned dissertation, Popper considers Hegel to be "the source of all contemporary historicism," and calls the historicism he adopted himself "a new tribalism," which, however, does not differ from the old one in the conviction that it is history that deals out the most important cards in what is now and what will be in the future, and people are, in fact, only cogs in this enormous machinery. This historicism differs from Plato's historicism, among others in the fact that in the opinion of the latter, "the trend of the development of the world of flux is a descent," while according to Hegel it is "an ascent" ("Hegel's historicism is optimistic"). Other elements of Hegelian historicism (such as the apology of totalitarianism and German nationalism) are only derived from this understanding of the world, including the understanding of the transformation of social life. Marxism (in Marx's original version) is here described as "a purely historical theory, a theory which aims at predicting the future course of economic and power-political developments and especially of revolutions," and at the same time as a philosophy of a revolt against the existing capitalist social relations – a rebellion, which is rational in the sense that in its justifications are aptly pointed out the injustice of social relations, and irrational in the sense that, in its tactics, it refers to emotions and takes advantage of emotions, but in its "final prophecies" envisages a situation in which after the victorious struggle of the workers and the bourgeoisie on the battlefield only the former will remain ("The bourgeoisie will disappear").[55]

---

[53] Cf. K. R. Popper, *Wiedza obiektywna. Ewolucyjna teoria epistemologiczna*, Warsaw 1992, p. 3.

[54] "It is an attitude which does not lightly give up hope that by such means as argument and careful observation, people may reach some kind of agreement on many problems of importance; and that, even where their demands and their interests clash, it is often possible to argue about the various demands and proposals, and to reach — perhaps by arbitration — a compromise which, because of its equity, is acceptable. To most, if not to all. In short, the rationalist attitude, or, as I may perhaps label it, the 'attitude of reasonableness', is very similar to the scientific attitude, to the belief that in the search for truth we need co-operation, and that, with the help of argument, we can in time attain something like objectivity." Cf. K. R. Popper, *The Open Society and Its Enemies*, Abindon 2005, p. 213.

[55] "The most likely development is, of course, that those actually in power at the moment of victory — those of the revolutionary leaders who have survived the struggle for power and

In the dissertation *The Poverty of Historicism*, Popper made a detailed analysis of this way of thinking and tried to show that "historicism is a poor method – a method which does not bear any fruit," and does not bear it, among other things, because historicists "deny that regularities detectable in social life have the character of the immutable regularities of the physical world," and also that the methods that have proved effective in the natural sciences cannot be applied in the study of social life (in their opinion, "in social sciences no really valuable experiments are possible").[56] To summarize, in this detailed and multi-faceted critique of historicism, Popper states that "[it] is a very old movement. Its oldest forms, such as the doctrines of the life cycles of cities and races, actually precede the primitive teleological view that there are hidden purposes behind the apparently blind decrees of fate [...]. Modern historicists, however, seem to be unaware of the antiquity of their doctrine. They believe – and what else could their deification of modernism permit? – that their own brand of historicism is the latest and boldest achievement of the human mind," i.e. that it is much more rational than anything that came before them. According to Popper, however, it is just as irrational as the earlier varieties, and its attractive-ness lies not in rationality, but not fully conscious emotionality, which grows out of fear of change – a fear "that prevents them from rational reaction to criticism." In this critique of historicism, Popper refers both to the history of human thought, and also operates a specific mode of thinking.

Some part of the answer to the question of what is and what expresses the specificity of Popperian historical thinking is contained in his *Objective of Knowledge*, particularly in the section entitled: *Evolutionary Epistemology*. However, its author does not draw a kind of historical fresco, presenting the evolution of philosophical thinking from subjectivism to contemporary forms of ob-jectivity, but presents the problems which, in his opinion, determine the most important points along this path. According to him, one problem is the ques-tion of induction. This has already been posed by ancient philosophers, but for modern discussions of greatest importance was its raising by D. Hume – he "was interested in the status of human knowledge or, as he might have said in the interesting question of whether any of our beliefs – and which of them – can be justified by sufficient reasons." What motivated Hume was this: "two problems: a logical problem (HL) and a psychological problem (Hps). One of the important points is that his two answers to these two problems in some

---

the various purges, together with their staff — will form a New Class: the new ruling class of the new society, a kind of new aristocracy or bureaucracy," and since they came to power thanks to preaching the abolition of class warfare, "it is most likely that they will attempt to hide this fact." Cf. ibidem, 127.

[56] Cf. K. R. Popper, *The Poverty of Historicism*, London 1957, p. 8 ff.

way clash with each other." As to the first problem, he argued that "we are not justified in reasoning from [repeated] instances of which we have experience to other instances [conclusions] of which we have no experience." As to the second, it is argued that the "great confidence" that lies in the fact that cases for which people have no experience "will conform to those of which they have experience," comes "out of custom or habit." In this way he showed that our knowledge is "unmasked as being not only of the nature of belief, but of rationally indefensible belief – of an irrational faith."[57] Beliefs are, of course, subjective. But knowledge about them can and should be objective. Hume himself could not solve this problem, however, and eventually became a sceptic, and a sceptic "who believed in irrationalistic epistemology," which – according to B. Russell – meant the "bankruptcy of the eighteenth-century reasonableness."[58]

In the next several paragraphs of this dissertation, Popper points out how to solve the problem of induction, or at least how he solves it. In the light of these arguments, generally this problem can be solved by (1) the translation of "all the subjective or psychological terms, especially 'belief,' etc., into *objective* terms, all subjective terms or psychological ones, especially 'convictions,' etc. to objective terms. [...] This procedure of putting things into the objective or logical or formal mode of speaking will be applied to HL, but not to HPs; however, (2) once the logical problem, HL, is solved, the solution is transferred to the psychological problem, HPs, on the basis of the following *principle of transference*: what is true in logic is true in psychology."[59] The appliance of this principle is not only "a guarantee of" the "elimination of Hume's irrationalism," but also of the elimination of other forms of irrationality that may appear on this path to objective knowledge. Components of this principle are: 1. "empirical reasons," i.e. recognition of the truth in these sentences of experience that sometimes "allow us to justify the claim that an explanatory universal theory is false;" 2. Preference for the theories "whose falsity has not been established;" 3. recognition of all rights or theories of a "hypothetical or conjectural" nature, i.e. considering them merely as "guesses."

"Once we have fully adopted this purely logical result, the question arises whether there can be purely rational arguments, including empirical arguments, for preferring some conjectures or hypotheses to others." Popper's answer to this question is a positive one, though he separates theoretical preferences and pragmatic preferences. In the case of the former, "the theoretician will therefore try his best to detect any false theory among the set of non-refuted

[57] Cf. K. R. Popper, *Objective Knowledge*, Oxford 1979, p. 5.

[58] Cf. B. Russell, *A History of Western Philosophy*, London 1946, p. 698 ff.

[59] "An analogous principle holds by and large for what is usually called 'scientific method', and also for the history of science..." Cf. K. R. Popper, *Objective Knowledge*, op. cit, p. 6.

competitors;" that is, "he will, with respect to any given non-refuted theory, try to think of cases or situations in which it is likely to fail, if it is false. Thus he will try to construct *severe* tests and *crucial* test situations."[60] He calls this method a critical one or – which is just the same – "the method of trial and elimination of error" through subjecting theories to "the possibly severest tests". This issue is solved differently by "a man of practical action," that is, the one who applies pragmatic preferences. Admittedly, he also faces the problem of rational choice, but in his behaviour he does not use the method of trial and elimination of error, but a method of the choice of the best tested theory. "The best tested theory is the one which, in the light of our critical discussion, appears to be the best so far, and I do not know of anything more 'rational' than a well-conducted critical discussion." In conclusion to this differentiation of preferences, Popper says that "there are many worlds, both possible and actual worlds, in which a searching for knowledge and for rules would fail." Even in such a world as the world of science in which relatively often "we achieve successes in our attempts to explain the world," such conditions occur in which searching for knowledge and achieving successes in this field "seems to be almost infinitely improbable."

In the section titled *Two Faces of Common Sense*, Popper poses and analyses the problem of common sense.[61] His starting hypothesis amounts to a statement that "science, philosophy, rational thought, must all start from common sense thinking – all this must have originated in common sense." However, in the past it was repeatedly questioned by the philosophy that is called "*scholastic*" – which had in common with scholasticism (without the quotation marks) that it challenged even the most "trivial theses of realism," such as the one claiming that "the world really exists." Popper by no means says that "common sense is a secure starting-point." On the contrary, referring to it gave and still gives legitimate reasons for criticism. It is only that this criticism cannot, and in any case should not, lead to a complete negation of the cognitive value of common sense. However, it should be "either modified by correction" or "transcended," but with such a correction and transcendence, in which "we must strive to remain faithful to the ideal: *All science, and all philosophy, are the enlightened common sense.*"[62] "The great tool" in this correction and transcendence

---

[60] "By this method of elimination, we may hit upon a true theory. But in no case can the method establish its truth, even if it is true; for the number of true theories remains infinite..." Cf. ibidem, p. 15.

[61] These "two faces of common sense" are, on the one hand, often attacked, by numerous philosophies, "naïve realism" (called by Popper "the bucket theory of the mind"), and on the other, critical and self-critical rationalism (often called "scientific rationalism"). The latter is connected with evolutionary epistemology.

[62] Cf. ibidem, p. 34.

of the weakness of common sense is – in the Popperian sense – proper critique and criticism, that is, one in which "we get a setting for rational discussion," and get it "when we explore the consequences of the theories, and when we try especially, to discover their weaknesses." However, its main component is to choose a proper starting point ("Descartes was perhaps the first to say that everything depends upon security of our starting-point of departure"), and the choice of the proper point of arrival (in Popper's interpretation this is constituted by theories which are made more probable than those of our predecessors). In an important addition to this thesis about making it more probable as the goal of science, Popper claims that "this is a more realistic goal than searching for truth or – "what Dewey called, *the quest for certainty*."

In the next few points of considerations on the scientific nature of common sense, Popper presents an outline of the *evolutionist epistemology*. In the light of these arguments, the idea of this epistemology was indeed born in the pre-Darwinian times, but the version proposed by Popper is "to some extent independent of those influences," and, of course, critical of the earlier evolutionary theory.[63] Its hallmarks are – of course, apart from the program of criticism and self-criticism – theses (hypotheses) stating that: 1. "the development of any knowledge consists in the modification of the previously existing knowledge," and "in the last resort consists in the modification of innate dispositions;" 2. "there is no reason to forbid us to conduct observational experiments by means of our provisional point of departure, which, like common sense, would imply commitment for truth and certainty." 3. there is subjective knowledge, which can be called "organismal knowledge" ("it is a kind of disposition of which an organism may sometimes realise in the form of a conviction, opinion or state of mind") and objective knowledge, which "consists of the logical content of our theories, conjectures, making out guesses, hypotheses, and if one wants from the logical content of his or her genetic code", but "we must be aware that at best we can only give a kind of sufficient correctness to a very, very small part of this knowledge to consider it as undoubtedly true" ("it contains statements of formal logic and finite arithmetic"); 4. "definitely the most important part of objective knowledge, including natural sciences – such as physics and physiology – is essentially of a hypothetical and suppositional character..." In the light of these claims (hypotheses) "the common-sense theory of knowledge remains essentially subjectivist" and the task of the philosopher and the scientist is not only to demonstrate this fact, but also such a proceeding which will lead to achieve maximum objectivity.[64]

---

[63] From the perspective of Popper's evolutionary epistemology, "a considerable part of Darwin is not of the nature of an empirical theory, but is a logical truism." Cf. ibidem, p. 69.

[64] "[...] we require that the believer should be in possession of sufficient reasons for establishing that the item of knowledge is true with certainty." Cf. ibidem, p. 75.

The "autocorrective method of science," i.e. "a method of bold hypotheses and inquisitive, and rigorous attempts to overthrow them" is to serve this purpose. These "bold hypotheses" or – what is just the same – "guesses," are "theories of rich content – at least richer than the theory we want to replace." However, these "probing and rigorous trials," the testing process, consist of "critical discussion, rational preference, and the problem of the analyticity of choices and predictions." "A critical discussion may never establish sufficient reasons", but with a bit of luck can give good reasons to the following statement: "At this moment this theory is in the light of a thorough critical discussion and severe and ingenious tests, by far the best (strongest, best checked), therefore it appears that among the competing theories, this theory is closest to truth."[65] At this point, Popper puts the equality sign between the concept of "rational" and the concept of "critical."

What this rationality (criticism) should look like in application is presented in the example of two competing hypotheses – h1 for Kepler's theory and h2 for Einstein's theory. Among other things, it indicates the conditions that must be fulfilled to be able to say that "it is rational to prefer h2 rather than h1," and "what happens when h2 is rationally preferable to h1." Basically, this preference will effect in the development of science, and it can also cause the motives for choosing Einstein's theory – "in contrast to the usual psychological motives" – to be "reasonably justifiable preferences" ("That is why logic and analytic sentences play such a great role in them"). However, it "cannot make this theory become true."[66] In conclusion to this example, he defines science as "the development of knowledge through creativity and criticism," and adds that he recognizes it as "one of the greatest achievements of the human mind," and also that "only science replaces elimination of errors in a violent struggle for existence by rational criticism without violence."

A vital complement to the vision of science and the standards of rationality connected with it is its conception of "worlds or universes: the first one is the world of objects or physical states, the second is the world of mental states or states of consciousness or behavioral dispositions to action, and the third, is the world of objective contents of thought, especially scientific and poetic thoughts and works of art."[67] Each of them is important in its own way, but from the standpoint of the philosopher and scientist seeking to achieve the objective knowledge is the most important, or at least the most desirable. This is confirmed both by "the Platonic theory of the world" and "Hegel's theory

---

[65] Cf. ibidem, p. 82.

[66] "They are at best logically inconclusive reasons for conjecturing that it is the most truthlike of the hypotheses competing at a certain time t." Cf. ibidem, p. 84.

[67] Cf. ibidem, p. 106.

of objective spirit," and even the theories of the "philosophers of convictions" (such as Descartes, Locke, Berkeley, Hume, Kant and Russell), who although they remained at the second level of these worlds, still they aspired to the third one. Answering the question of what exists in the third world, Popper points out "primarily *the theoretical systems*, but equally important objects are problems and problem situations." After having a closer look at these "inhabitants," it appears that the most important in it are "critical arguments, and that which, by analogy to physical state or states of consciousness can be called *states of discussion or states of critical argumentation*; and, of course, the contents of journals, books and libraries."[68]

What is important is not only who inhabits this third world, but also how it is created. According to Popper, it is created in a way "relatively independent" of the first and second worlds. To justify this general thesis, he presents two thought experiments – in the light of the first experiment, this world will not cease to exist even if "all machines and tools were destroyed," and in the light of the second one, it will not cease to exist even when "our subjective knowledge with the subjective knowledge of machines and tools and the ways of using them is destroyed." What is also important is how this third world is studied and how it should not be studied. As to this issue, Popper formulated three general theses: "The first one is as follows: traditional epistemology explored knowledge or ideas explored in the subjective sense," "the second thesis says that for epistemology an essential matter is the study of scientific problems and problem situations," while the third says that "objectivist epistemology, which studies the third world, throws a great deal of light on the second world of subjective consciousness, especially on the subjective thought processes of scientists." A rationalization for these theses is supposedly: 1. "the biological theory of the third world" (it says that "the third world is a natural product of the human animal"), 2. the "considerable autonomy of the world", and 3. the thesis which claims that "thanks to the interaction between us ('the inhabitants of the first and second world') and the third world, objective knowledge is growing and that there is a close analogy between the development of knowledge and biological development, i.e. the evolution of plants and animals."

In the detailed comments to these theses, Popper points out, among other things, the way in which this autonomy is created. Generally, it is supposed to be created through posing new or partly new problems, making attempts at solving them by framing bold hypotheses, subjecting them to "critical discussion or experimental tests," and arriving at a new problem situation, which differs from the previous one in that the number of the possibilities has been

---

[68] Cf. ibidem, p. 107.

narrowed by the elimination of those that were admitted in the initial problem situation, and which have not passed the test of "critical discussion or experimental tests." He also indicates language as "the most important invention of man," which makes that the human mind is capable of performing such higher functions as a description of the world and argumentation.[69] In addition to this recognition of language as a factor distinguishing man in the world of living beings a statement appears that "we owe our humanity, our intellect to the development of the higher functions of language. The power of reasoning is nothing more than the power of critical argumentation." As the lower functions of language, Popper considers the functions of communication and those of expression. Therefore, it can be assumed that in the Popperian epistemology – called by the author of The *Objective Knowledge* – "epistemology without a knowing subject," the function of the subject is taken over by such a language in which the world is described and critical arguments are formulated. Assigning this function to language is a specific kind of crowning of the Popperian conception of rationality. The rest can be considered as additions to it. In any case, Popper seems to treat this "rest" in such a way himself.

It should also be said that within the standards of reality adopted by him, the concept of *addition* takes on a particular meaning.[70] This can be seen especially in his *Conjectures and Refutations: The Growth of Scientific Knowledge*. In the introduction to its first English edition *conjectures* are defined as contributing to the development of knowledge ("especially the scientific one") "unjustified (and unjustifiable) anticipations, test solutions," while *refutations* are involved with submitting the former to "attempts at refuting/rejecting through stringent tests". Popper combines the two steps of conjectures and refutations with "a theory of reason that assigns to rational arguments the modest and yet important role of criticizing our often mistaken attempts to solve our problems."[71] It can be assumed that this "anticipation and adoption of test solutions," and then submitting them to attempts at refutation is the very nucleus of the way

---

[69] "The argumentative function of human language assumes its descriptive function: arguments generally are concerned with descriptions: they submit those descriptions to criticism from the perspective of regulatory ideas of truth, content, and probability."

[70] Obviously, this does not mean that this narration and argumentation HAS equivalents in the philosophical tradition. Without much effort one can point to masters of such insertions as Erasmus of Rotterdam or M. Montaigne. A special place among them is occupied by Descartes with such an important addition to his *Meditation on First Philosophy* as the *Accusations of Learned Men* and author's replies. This particular work of Descartes has two considerable addenda in the form of Poincaré's *Value of Science* and the *Cartesian Meditations* of Husserl.

[71] "And it is a theory of experience that assigns to our observations the equally modest and almost equally important role of tests which may help us in the discovery of our mistakes." Cf. K. R. Popper, *Conjectures and Refutations, The Growth of Scientific Knowledge*, New York 1962, p. vi.

of arriving at objective knowledge, which he postulated and accepted It is not only acceptable, but even inevitable and indeed justified here to put the same problem forward repeatedly, and to repeat attempts at refuting the accepted theses, hypotheses and theories – including those that "appear to be highly resistant to criticism and which, at some point in time, seem to be better approximations to truth than the other ones." The rationalization of this repeated posing of the same problems is the Popperian thesis that in science none of the proposed solutions can be considered as "ultimately justified." Of course, this opens an extensive area for these *additions*, which are a sort of subsequent approximation to truth – or for correction of the previous approximations, or for indicating in it such an aspect of that truth (which could be both some proposed solution and some problem situation), which was not previously identified, described and subjected to critical analysis.

The vast majority of the problems posed and the solutions proposed in this work have their own appendices ("containing some perhaps useful observations on these issues"). And so, in the appendix to the discussion of the point titled – *Science: Conjectures and Refutations*, Popper presented selected "problems of the philosophy of science" (including those related to the theory of probability, operationalism and instrumentalism, explanations, etc.). In the appendix to the point of discussion titled – *Back to Presocratics* – Popper responds to the criticism of "Mr. Kirk" from the article *Popper on Science and the Presocratics* (in the light of the argument found there, "that which Kirk considers to be the Popperian 'attitude to the methodology of science', is based on misconceptions and erroneous reading of his text"). Finally, in the addition to the point entitled – *Truth, Rationality and the Development of Knowledge* – he speaks of "the probably false, but still formally highly probable, non-empirical sentences" (Popper includes among them metaphysical sentences).

All this is found in the part presenting the *Conjectures*. However, in the part detailing the *Refutations* there are no explicit additions; this is due to the fact that this part of the book is in itself such an addition to the Popperian conception of objective knowledge and the standards of rationality connected with it. *Conjectures* contain a polemic with Carnap's reasonableness and unreasonableness (a theory already criticised by Popper in his *Logic of Scientific Discovery*), and with Hegelian and post-Hegelian "predictions and prophecies in the social sciences" (already criticised in *An Open Society and Its Enemies*). The whole of this work is completed with *Additions*, of course, also including additions to the previously presented additions, but also to that which is found in *The Objective Knowledge*, among others, including such problems as the problem of "probability against severity of tests," or the problem of "artificial and formalised languages."

It is also worth taking a closer look at the function of these additions in *The Objective Knowledge*, where only several are described as *additions*. Such, for example, is the case with the part titled by Popper *A Behavioral Mutant* (which is an addition to the part titled *Evolution and the Tree of Knowledge*), and with the additions closing the considerations contained in the book, the first titled: *A Bucket and a Searchlight* (containing an addition to the so-called "bucket theory of knowledge"), and the second, under the title *Supplementary Remarks* (which among other things, contain "responses to some of the criticisms directed against the views presented in this book since its publication in 1972"). However, part of the considerations titled *Once Again about Induction* also has some of the characteristics of an addition (it was placed after *The Two Faces of Common Sense* and contains an important addition on the question of the "critical analysis of the philosophy of common sense") as well as part of *The Clouds and Clocks* (placed after the presentation "theory of objective mind", and "the goal of science" and containing "an outline of the theory of rationality and human freedom").[72]

Postscript

The issue that appears in all the works of Popper quoted here is his attitude, on the one hand, to philosophical tradition, which he called *idealism, apriorism* or *deductionism* and, on the other hand, to the tradition called by him *realism, empiricism* or *inductionism*. One might have the impression that Poppers shifts from one to the other on different occasions. Much depends here on the context of the problems in which they are called upon. However, there is no doubt that he is critical of both, and his evolutionary epistemological theory is by assumption supposed to assume everything that is rational in each of them and to propose such standards of rationality that the mistakes and shortcomings of his philosophical predecessors would be corrected.

In *The Objective Knowledge,* both traditions are mentioned and subjected to criticism. Primary focus is given to the tradition of realism and the tradition of inductivism associated with it. The former is referred to only occasionally, mainly in connection with its absurd theses, such as, for example, the one stating "the world is just a dream." Directly opposite is the naive realism, which is expressed in a common-sense belief that the world really exists, or, that reality

---

[72] "My clouds are intended to represent physical systems which, like gases, are highly irregular, disorderly, and more or less unpredictable [...]. On the other extreme of our arrangement, on its right, we may place a very reliable pendulum clock, a precision clock, intended to represent physical systems which are regular, orderly, and highly predictable in their behaviour." Cf. K. R. Popper, *Objective Knowledge*, op. cit., p. 207.

is so real that its existence would not be questioned by anybody in their right mind. And therein lies the problem, because "all the arguments for this belief are based on a non-critical acceptance of common sense." There were attempts in the past to cope with this, but even those who, like Hume ("the most reasonable thinker of all time"), were able to indicate that those arguments in favour are not logical reasons, but are rather psychological "reasons" (if we can call habits, customs and associations reasons) would finally come across paradoxes and the denial of human rationality.[73] All in all, the argumentation contained in *The Objective Knowledge* aims to show the weaknesses of common-sense realism and its oppositions which concluded in the "theories of subjective reason" or – which is just the same thing – came to the limits of the other world, i.e., the world of subjective consciousness and were not capable of overcoming these limits. Of course, the work shows not only the weaknesses of traditional realism (and the inductivism associated with it), but also the possibilities of their rational transgressing and entering the third world. In sum, the generalizations which appear there still leave a number of doubts concerning Popper's attitude both towards cognitive realism and idealism.

His *Conjectures and Refutations: the Roads to Knowledge* contains answers to at least some of these doubts. Among others things, it has a critical presentation of the viewpoint of Carnap's logical empiricism. The list of accusations against him is diverse. These accusations support the general thesis saying that the "attempts, repeatedly made by Rudolf Carnap, to show that the boundary between science and metaphysics coincides with the demarcation line separating meaningful utterances from meaningless ones, failed;" they failed, among other things, because "the positivist conception of "meaning" or "sense" (verifiability or induction) does not allow to demarcate this limit: metaphysics need not be a nonsense, even if it is not science."[74] This general thesis is accompanied not only by justification, but also by a general statement saying that the aim of science (and the scientists' activity) "is not to achieve a high logical probability of propositions or theories," but their "high semantic content," and the latter grows "with the increasing degree of verifiability." The problem lies not in the fact that Carnap denied the importance of verifiability in science (on the contrary, he recognized it as a condition of the scientific character of theorems formulated in it), but in the fact that in the light of his assumptions and postulates: 1. their verification occurs through confirmation (showing their truthfulness); 2. "on the strength of his definition of the degree of verifiability the laws of nature appear to be unconfirmable;" and

---

[73] In Hume this is expressed as seeing and presenting man not as "a rational being, but rather a product of blind habit". Cf. K. R. Popper, *Objective Knowledge*, op. cit., p. 95.

[74] Cf. K. R. Popper, *Conjectures and Refutations...*, op. cit., p. 253.

3. the highest degree of verifiability may prove to be the protocol propositions (such as: "Here is a glass of water") and the ones that can be reduced to
such propositions. ("This excludes from the class of meaningful statements
all scientific theories because they are also equally irreducible to protocol sentences as the so-called metaphysical pseudosentences"). Popper shows here
that Carnap, while fighting metaphysics and metaphysicism in science, adopts
metaphysical assumptions himself – if only the assumption of the possibility
(and necessity) of the "translatability of everything I say (in philosophy and
science – A/N) into a formal way of speaking" ("Why should it be exactly like
this? Is it because the *essence* of philosophy is the analysis of language?"). In
his conclusions of this criticism, Popper states that in Carnap's logical empiricism there is a breaking off from the principle of empiricism, and some of
its assumptions and postulates "make the impression of being an acceptance
to some extent of the *aprioristic* standpoint."

His *Conjectures and Refutations: The Growth of Scientific Knowledge* contains
a series of references to the previously published (1934) *The Logic of Scientific
Discovery*. There is not only a series of expanding additions to the criticism
of Carnap's standpoint and of other members of the Vienna Circle, but also
a critical analysis of the scientist and philosopher H. Poincaré's standpoint,
who at that time was considered to be one of the leading representatives
of conventionalism in the philosophy of science, while at the same time he
was a follower of that tradition of philosophy which derives from Plato, and
subsequently has its important representatives in the persons of Descartes,
Leibniz and Kant.[75]

According to Popper, "the source of the conventionalist philosophy is
the astonishment with the raw beauty of the world as shown in the laws of
physics. Surely, conventionalists nurse the feeling that this simplicity would be
an inconceivable miracle if we followed the realists and believed that the laws
of nature reveal an internal structural simplicity of the world hiding under
the external manifestations of wasteful diversity. Kant's idealism sought to
explain this simplicity, claiming that this is just our reason that imposes its
laws on nature. A conventionalist similarly, and even more courageously, treats
simplicity as our own creation. According to him, the simplicity of nature is
not the result of laws of our reason imposed on nature, because he does not
believe at all that nature is simple. Simple are only the laws of nature, which, as
a conventionalist would maintain, are our own, arbitrary creations, our inventions, arbitrary resolutions and conventions. For a conventionalist theoretical

---

[75] Its competitive traditions are marked by such names as Bacon, Hobbes, Locke, Hume
and Mill, and as its leading representative Popper considers B. Russell. Cf. K. R. Popper, *Logic
of Scientific Discovery*, London 2002, p. xxii.

natural sciences do not reflect nature, because they are only logical constructs. These constructs are not determined by the properties of the world, but just the contrary, it is just those constructs which determine the properties of an artificial world: the world of concepts implicitly defined by the laws of nature selected by us. Science speaks only about such a world." However, a little further he adds that "the manner in which conventionalist philosophy has helped to explain the relationships between theory and experiment deserves recognition" and also that "he considers conventionalism as a coherent and good system. It is rather unlikely that it will be possible to detect any contradictions in it."[76]

What Popper accuses conventionalists of is that they "expect ultimate certainty in science," or, in other words, that they seek in science "a system of knowledge based upon ultimate grounds." According to him, "this goal is attainable; for it is possible to interpret any given system of science as a system of implicit definitions" – definitions implicated in language, traditions, old and new systems, hypotheses etc. In the further parts of his considerations he concentrates not so much on these entanglements as on an attempt at articulating such methodological rules, which would supposedly not allow to "finally solve the dispute with conventionalists about the status of scientific theories (systems)", nevertheless, they would allow to point to the need and possibility of their falsifiability (showing their falseness). To this end he first presents "a logical investigation of falsifiability" and its results, such as, among other things, the distinction of "a system of basic statements" ("the system of base sentences is to contain all the internally non-contradictory singular statements of a definite logical form") or the formulation of "the demand that the theory should allow us to deduce, roughly speaking, more empirical singular statements than we can deduce from the initial conditions alone". These statements are premises to the statement that 1. "a theory is falsified only if we have accepted basic sentences which contradict it; 2. "we only accept the falsification if a low-level empirical hypothesis, which describes such an effect is proposed and corroborated". Therefore, we have two conditions for the acceptance of scientific theories (systems), i.e., the condition of non-contradiction and the condition of the possibility of showing falseness (falsifiability).[77]

---

[76] Cf. ibidem, p. 58. This author considers Poincaré to be an advocate of "the principle of selection of theories" ("selection of simplest conventions"); however, not treated as a certain version of falsificationism ("a conventionalist does not treat theories as falsifiable systems, but rather as conventional statements").

[77] "The two conditions are to a large extent analogous. Statements which do not satisfy the condition of consistency fail to differentiate between any two statements within the totality of all possible statements. Statements which do not satisfy the condition of falsifiability fail to differentiate between any two statements within the totality of all possible empirical basic statements." Cf. ibidem, p. 73.

I am inclined to claim that this standpoint is closer to Poincaré than Popper's original thought. It is because his thesis saying that, according to a conventionalist, "the laws of science" are merely "our own, arbitrary creations, our inventions, our arbitrary resolutions and conventions" is not confirmed in *The Value of Science*. Therefore, I shall recall that its author not only maintained that these (and similar) "delicate constructions [...] are totally mind-made," but also point to the rules that guide the scientist in their "deriving." While answering the question of what guides the scientists in the adoption thereof, he pointed not only to the convenience and simplicity, but also, on the one hand, to the "compulsion of empiricism" (as proponents of empiricism would say) and, on the other, the necessity of deducing such logical consequences of general statements which would enable to apply to nature a logical "yes or no" question, and it can be reasonably expected that nature would give the scientist a satisfactory answer to this question. It is also worth reminding that in the light of Poincaré's standpoint neither this "yes" nor this "no" gives or can give a scientist "the ultimate certainty" – at most, it can give greater certainty than the one he had had before when attempting to solve the problem he had posed. Of course, what is important here is not only who is asked, but also who asks and how he asks. If that person is a scientist, then he has the proper "mandate" (if his qualifications can be called this way) to ask daring questions and to formulate even the most risky hypotheses. In this respect there is no radical difference between Popper and Poincaré.

Bibliography

Adam A. et all, *Literatura francuska*, t. I, PWN, Warsaw 1974.

Aristotle, *Ethics*, Pennsylvania State University, Pennsylvania 2004.

Aristotle, *The Works of Aristotle: Organon or Logical Treatises of Aristotle*, Prometheus Trust, Cornell University, New York 2001.

Aristotle, *Works*, Clarendon Press, Oxford 1956.

Augustine, *Against the academicians and The Teacher,* Hackett Publishing Co., Indianapolis 1995.

Augustyn W., *Podstawy wiedzy u Descartes'a i Malebranche'a*, PWN, Warsaw 1973.

Buczyńska-Garewicz H., *Koło Wiedeńskie. Początek neopozytywizmu*, Wiedza Powszechna, Warsaw 1960.

Buksiński T., *Dwa rozumy filozofii*, in: idem, *Rozumność i racjonalność*, Wydawnictwo Naukowe Instytutu Filozofii UAM, Poznan 1997.

Carnap R., *Philosophy and Logical Syntax*, Kegan Paul, Trench, Trubner & Co., London London 1935.

Comte A., *A General View of Positivism*, Routledge, London 1908.

Descartes, *Discourse on the Method*, Cosimo, New York 2008.

Descartes, *Meditations on First Philosophy*, Oxford University Press, Oxford 2008.

Descartes, *Principles of Philosophy*, in: *The philosophical writings of Descartes*, vol. 1, Cambridge University Press, Cambridge 1985.

Descartes, *Rules for the Direction of the Mind*, in: *The philosophical writings of Descartes*, vol. 1, Cambridge University Press, Cambridge 1985.

Diogenes Laertius, *Lives and Opinions of Eminent Philosophers*, George Bell and Sons, London 1895.

Drozdowicz Z., *Kartezjusz a współczesność*, Wydawnictwo Naukowe UAM, Poznan 1980.

Drozdowicz Z., *Les Meditations cartesiennes d'Henri Poincare*, in: *L'esprit cartésien, Actes du XXVIe Congres de l'Association de Philosophie de Langue Francaise*, edites par: B. Bourgeois et J. Hevet, Paris 2000.

Elberfeld R., *Was ist Philosophie? Programmatische Texte von Platon bis Derrida*, Philipp Reclam, Stuttgart 2006.

Erasmsus, *Colloquies*, Reeves and Turner, Chicago 1878.

Erasmus, *Colloquies*, vol. 1, University of Toronto Press, Toronto 1997.

Erasmus, *The Praise of Folly*, Peter Eckler Publishing Co., New York 1922.

Erazm z Rotterdamu, *Sposób, czyli metoda szybkiego i łatwego dochodzenia do prawdziwej teologii*, in: *Trzy rozprawy*, PAX, Warsaw 1960.

Gassendi P., *Fifth Replies*, in: Descartes, *Meditations on First Philosophy*, Oxford University Press, Oxford 2008.

Gilson E., *History of Christian Philosophy in the Middle Ages*, Sheed and Ward, London 1980.

Gilson E., *The Unity of Philosophical Experience*, Charles Schribners Sons, New York 1950.

Hegel G. W. F., *Encyclopedia of the Philosophical Sciences in Basic Outline*, Cambridge, Cambridge University Press, 2010.

Hegel G. W. F., *Lectures on the History of Philosophy*, Humanites Press, London 1892-1896.

Hegel G. W. F., *Phenomenology of Spirit*, Oxford University Press, Oxford 1977.

Hegel G. W. F., *Philosophy of the mind*, Cosimo, New York 2008.

Hegel G. W. F., *Philosophy of Right*, Cosimo, New York 2008.

Hegel G. W. F., *Science of logic*, G. Allen & Unwin, London 1969.

Hegel G. W. F., *The Philosophy of History*, Batoche Books, Ontario 2001.

Huizinga J., *The Waning of the Middle Ages*, Penguin Books, London 1987.

Husserl E., *Cartesian Meditations*, 7th Impression, Martinus Nijhoff, The Hague 1982.

Kant I., *Critique of Practical Reason*, Dover, New York 1954.

Kant I., *Critique of Pure Reason*, Dover Publications Inc., New York 2004.

Kołakowski L., *Filozofia pozytywistyczna. Od Hume'a do Koła Wiedeńskiego*, PWN, Warsaw 1966.

Kondylis P., *Die Aufklärung im Rahmen des neuzeitlichen Rationalismus*, Klett-Cotta, Stuttgart 1981.

Kristeller P. O., *Renesans w historii myśli filozoficznej*, in: idem, *Humanizm i filozofia*, PAN, Institut Filozofii i Socjologii, Warsaw 1985

Kroński T., *Kant*, Wiedza Powszechna, Warsaw 1966.

Le Goff J., *Intellectuals in the Middle Ages*, Blackwell, Oxford 1993.

Legowicz J., *Zarys historii filozofii*, Wiedza Powszechna, Warsaw 1967.

Leszczyński D., Szlachcic K., *Wprowadzenie do francuskiej filozofii nauki*, Wydawnictwo Uniwersytetu Wrocławskiego, Wroclaw 2003.

Leśniak K., *Platon*, Wiedza Powszechna, Warsaw 1968.

Letter to J. S. Mill (of June 19, 1842), in: A. Comte, *Correspondance inedite*, vol. 1, Au Siège de la Société Positiviste, Paris 1903.

Montaigne M., *Essays*, vol. 1, Reeves & Turner, London 1902.

Montaigne M., *The Complete Essays of Michel de Montaigne*, vol. 2, London 1910.

Nicholas of Cusa, *On Learned Ignorance*, Minneapolis, Arthur J. Banning Press, Minneapolis, 1985.

Pascal B., *Thoughts*, P. F. Collier and Son, New York 1910.

Paź B., *Naczelna zasada racjonalizmu. Od Kartezjusza do wczesnego Kanta*, Auireus, Cracow 2007.

Plato, *Meno*, Ferenity Publishers, Rockville 2009.

Plato, *Parmenides*, Echo Library, Teddington 2006.

Plato, *Phaedo*, in: *Plato's Apology, Crito and Phaedo*, D. McKay, Philadelphia 1897.

Plato, *Philebus*, in: *Three Dialogues: Protagoras, Philebus, and Gorgias*, Oxford University Press, New York 2011.

Plato, *The Apology of Socrates*, in: *Plato's Apology, Crito and Phaedo*, D. McKay, Philadelphia 1897.

Plato, *The Republic*, Basic Books, New York 1991.

Plato, *Timaeus*, in: *Timaeus and Critias*, Digireads.com Publishing 2009.

Plotinus, *Six Enneads*, Kessinger Publishing, Whitefish 2004.

Poincaré H., *Science and Hypothesis*, in: *The Foundations of Science*, The Science Press, New York 1913.

Poincaré H., *Science and Method*, in: *The Foundations of Science*, The Science Press, New York 1913.

Poincaré H., *The Value of Science*, in: idem, *The Foundations of Science*, The Science Press, New York 1913.

Popper K. R., *Conjectures and Refutations, The Growth of Scientific Knowledge*, Basic Books, New York 1962.

Popper K. R., *Logic of Scientific Discovery*, Routledge, London 2002.

Popper K. R., *Objective Knowledge*, Clarendon Press, Oxford 1979.

Popper K. R., *The Open Society and Its Enemies*, Routledge, Abindon 2005.

Popper K. R., *The Poverty of Historicism*, Routledge&Kegan Paul, London 1957.

Popper K. R., *Wiedza obiektywna. Ewolucyjna teoria epistemologiczna*, Wydawnictwo Naukowe PWN, Warsaw 1992.

Reale G., *A History of Ancient Philosophy. I: From the Origins to Socrates*, SUNY Press, Albany 1987.

Reale G., *A History of Ancient Philosophy II: Plato and Aristotle*, SUNY Press, Albany 1990.

Reichenbach H., *The rise of scientific philosophy*, University of California Press, Berkeley 1951.

Rodis-Lewis G., *Kartezjusz i racjonalizm*, Prószyński i S-ka, Warsaw 2000.

Russell B., *A History of Western Philosophy*, Allen&Unwin, London 1946.

Schnädelbach H., *Próba rehabilitacji animal rationale*, Oficyna Naukowa, Warsaw 2001.

Schnädelbach H., *Rozum i historia*, Oficyna Naukowa, Warsaw 1994.

Siemek M., *Hegel: Rozum i historia*, in: idem, *W kręgu filozofów*, Czytelnik, Warsaw 1984.

Skarga B., *Kłopoty intelektu. Między Comte'em a Bergsonem*, PWN, Warsaw 1975.

Spink J. S., *French Free-Thought from Gassendi to Voltaire*, The Athlone Press of the University of London, London 1960.

Szahaj A., *Postmodernizm a scjentyzm*, in: *Kultura jako przedmiot badań. Studia filozoficzno-kulturoznawcze*, Wydawnictwo Fundacji Humaniora, Poznan 2001.

Weischedel W., *Die philosophische Hintertreppe. Die grossen Philosophen in Alltag und Denken*, Nymphenburger Verlagshandlung GmbH, Munich 1973.

Whittaker T., *The Neo-Platonists*, Cambridge University Press, London 1928.

Index of persons

* References to footnotes are in italics.